THE CULTURE *of* HEAVEN

INFUSING YOUR WORLD WITH THE REALITY OF THE SUPERNATURAL

TROY GOODE

WHITAKER HOUSE

The Culture of Heaven:
Infusing Your World with the Reality of the Supernatural

Troy Goode
42326 Albrae St.
Fremont, CA 94538
http://whpub.whitakerhouse.com/cultureofheaven/index.html

ISBN: 978-1-64123-044-5
eBook ISBN: 978-1-62911-580-1
Printed in the United States of America

Whitaker House
1030 Hunt Valley Circle
New Kensington, PA 15068
www.whitakerhouse.com

Library of Congress Cataloging-in-Publication Data (Pending)

1 2 3 4 5 6 7 8 9 10 11 WH 25 24 23 22 21 20 19 18

What Others Are Saying About *The Culture of Heaven*

"While many people are talking about God's will being done on earth as it is in heaven, few people actually have given us a 'how-to' road map. Pastor Troy has done us all a favor in helping us fulfill our role as believers. *The Culture of Heaven* is extremely well-written and will change your life."

—*Cindy Jacobs*
Cofounder, Generals International

"Jesus reproved Nicodemus, who came to him by night undercover for fear of the religious elite he was a part of, and was instructed by the Savior about the move of the Spirit and the purposes of God in Christ. Jesus told him, 'The wind blows where it wills, and you hear the sound of it, but you don't know where it comes from or where it is going.' (See John 3:8.) Nicodemus didn't know what he was supposed to know because he was figuratively 'in the dark.' Too many believers remain 'in the dark' about the activities and movement of the Spirit. My dear friend Troy Goode sheds needful light on the culture of heaven in these days of a fresh outpouring of the wind and breath of God upon the nations."

—*Dr. Mark Chironna*
Pastor, Church on the Living Edge
Founder, Mark Chironna Ministries

"Wow! This is more than a book, it's a celestial travel guide! Troy Goode has given us an antidote to 'end time' anxiety. If we all practiced what Troy teaches we would see a viral move of God planting lush gardens of heaven in the midst of a scorched earth. Once people taste *The Culture of Heaven,* they will never be happy with a counterfeit. I encourage you to read it!"

—*Lance Wallnau*
Lance Learning Group

"This is not a book on theory. It goes way beyond that and clearly demonstrates how biblical principles can come to life in a real church in a real city. Troy Goode does a remarkable job of showing how heaven's culture can materialize here on earth. You will love this book! It is a message we all need today."

—*The late C. Peter Wagner*
Former Chancellor Emeritus, Wagner Leadership Institute

"For more than three decades, my own church has been on a passionate pursuit of God's presence. This pursuit has preconditioned us to recognize others who share in that same quest. *The Culture of Heaven* is a chronicle of one who has had the privilege of participating in that journey."

—*Bishop Joseph L. Garlington Sr.*
Senior Pastor, Covenant Church of Pittsburgh
Presiding Bishop, Reconciliation! Ministries International

"I'm in pursuit of the presence of God these days like never before. So I praise God for this book, written from the heart of a fellow pursuer. If you have a sincere desire to experience God in a fresh way, you'll be inspired, enlightened, and challenged by *The Culture of Heaven*."

—*Paul Sheppard*
Host, *Destined for Victory* radio program

DEDICATION

I dedicate this book to my fathers and mentors. I have lived with such a deep sense of responsibility all my life because I've been surrounded by incredible men who have poured themselves into me at various seasons. Thank you to Malvin Goode, Ché Ahn, Bill Johnson, Bishop Gideon Thompson, Bishop Joseph Garlington, Ronn Elmore, Mark Stibbe, Pastor Paul Sheppard, and one who has stood with me at every season of life—my dad, Pastor Richard Allen Goode. I love you all so much.

CONTENTS

Foreword....9
Introduction....13
1. More than You Bargained For....19
2. Hardwired for the Supernatural....39
3. Paying for Your Oil....57
4. Use It or Lose It....77
5. Hanging Out with the Anointing....95
6. Private Life, Public Breakthrough....115
7. Have a Drink on Us!....141
8. Power Giving....157
Conclusion....173
About the Author....175

FOREWORD

In our world, culture invades every aspect of life. We are vulnerable to its many facets, all of them shaping and molding our belief systems. Culture dictates and governs how the world, and everyone in it, will operate.

Merriam-Webster's Dictionary supplies the following definition for *culture*: "the customary beliefs, social forms, and material traits of a racial, religious, or social group;...the characteristic features of everyday existence (such as diversions or a way of life) shared by people in a place or time; the set of shared attitudes, values, goals, and practices that characterizes an institution or organization." As believers in Christ, we need to be governing the earth with the kingdom of heaven in mind more than the dictates of the society in which we live.

Jesus instructs us, *"In this manner, therefore, pray: Our Father in heaven, hallowed be Your name. Your kingdom come. Your will be done on earth as it is in heaven"* (Matthew 6:9–10). So, how do we get His kingdom and His will from heaven to earth?

My spiritual son Troy Goode and I have many things in common, but the one thing that stands out the most to me is our unwavering commitment to pursuing the presence of God and maintaining an open heaven for the Holy Spirit to move freely. Such an atmosphere is where things that seem impossible or unlikely will happen—where you will be able to impact your surroundings and influence your culture.

Troy has done an outstanding job in writing *Culture of Heaven: Finding and Keeping the Manifest Presence of God.* This book is laden with powerful truths and thought-provoking stories that will move you from a position of "status quo" to a deep hunger for God's presence. Troy is open, honest, and humble as he willingly shares his personal experiences and testimonies to give you hope, belief, and faith that you, too, can have deeper fellowship with God. Out of this place of intimacy with the Father flow His love and character. You become more like Him, and His very nature begins to exude from you.

Some people think that experiencing the supernatural things of heaven and bringing them down to earth require a special calling, a seminary degree, or a generational inheritance from your family line operating in the supernatural. But the reality is that our loving heavenly Father hungers to be with you and to pour out His goodness in your life. Troy gives practical tools that will help you engage with heaven. The examples included in this book will help you see differently, with a fresh perspective that will even equip you to apply your own experiences to furthering your relationship with God.

There are many powerful statements and facts in this book that will cause you to reassess your level of intimacy with the Father, reevaluate your belief system, and open your understanding of God's original blueprint for the earth. Troy has penned some amazing statements that will compel you to stop and reread that which caught your spirit. Here is one that had that effect on me: "In heaven, the culture is right-side up, and God's Word is the Rosetta Stone that unlocks the mysteries of life there. It's our world, as we've come to know it, that's upside down."

Troy has hungered for and sought the manifest presence of God with great passion and intentionality. He has laid down his life to be more like Jesus and has taken on a lifestyle of intimate communion with the Father. He has cultivated a relationship with the Holy Spirit. But all of this has not come without a price. Troy had endured much tribulation, which no one likes to go through, but his hunger to flow in the anointing has pressed him into God. And now the Lord God has entrusted him to write this book filled with heavenly revelation and insight gained from his journey with his "Abba, Father."

In the pages of this book, you will understand how to get God's kingdom and God's will from heaven to earth. Prepare to have your life impacted in such a way that your relationship with Jesus will go intimately deeper, His manifest presence will be evident in your life, and heaven will be released through you to influence the culture around you!

—*Dr. Ché Ahn*

Apostle, Harvest Apostolic Center

Founding Pastor, HRock Church, Pasadena, CA

President, Harvest International Ministry

INTRODUCTION

A revelation received creates an atmosphere; an atmosphere sustained creates a climate; a climate sustained becomes a stronghold; a stronghold sustained creates a culture; and a culture influences the world.

Most people don't recognize this pattern, which is highlighted by celebrated author Malcolm Gladwell in his classic book *The Tipping Point,* and yet they are impacted by it regularly. Gladwell's premise is that ideas can develop into large-scale movements when even a small number of people become "infected" by the original concept. With that type of momentum, something that begins as a mere idea embraced by a few passionate people can go viral and infect an entire culture, creating an epidemic!

Let's consider an example. In the United States, the homosexual community makes up approximately 3 percent of the population. Yet a Gallup poll conducted in 2011 indicated that most Americans, at the time, believed the homosexual community to compose closer to 25 percent of the nation's population. Regardless of your position on homosexuality, you cannot deny the way in which a relatively small number of people have managed to change the perspective of an entire nation. The influence of the homosexual community has caused an entire culture to imagine that homosexual people are more numerous than they really are.

Hip-hop music is another example. The style was born in the deprived Bronx section of New York City, where a few kids with no access to instruments started making music. Today, hip-hop has become a global phenomenon.

What enabled these minority groups to develop such momentum and pulling power? In a word, "culture." The members of these micro-movements consciously or unconsciously found a way to sustain their idea until other people became carriers of the same message. Sooner or later, those messages hit a critical mass and started to develop their own look, values, style, vernacular, and feeling. And all those elements ultimately combined to create a culture.

Cultures are powerful because they define normative behavior for a specific people group, city, state, region, or nation. Culture tells people what to think. It also makes people believe that what they are saying and doing is legitimate and positive, because they are made to feel that everyone else around them is thinking, believing, saying, and doing the same things.

In the realm of the Christian church, there are distinct cultures, usually defined along denominational lines. If you're a Baptist, there's a "Baptist way" of doing things. The same goes if you're a Methodist. Catholics even have their own vernacular and vocabulary—terms such as "sacrament," "Holy See," and "basilica"—that few people outside the Catholic Church would ever use. Within Catholicism, however, these words are integral parts of the culture.

This book is all about cultural norms. But it isn't talking about the norms of a national culture, a business culture, or even an artistic or religious culture. This book is about the *culture of heaven*. In the model prayer Jesus gave to us in the Gospels, He directed us to pray that what is experienced in heaven should be experienced on earth. So, what's it like in heaven? What are the cultural norms of heaven? What language, style, and feeling does heaven embody?

IN THE MODEL PRAYER JESUS GAVE TO US IN THE GOSPELS, HE DIRECTED US TO PRAY THAT WHAT IS EXPERIENCED IN HEAVEN SHOULD BE EXPERIENCED ON EARTH.

The heart of Father God is for His people to be influenced daily by the same culture that He has created and now inhabits. Moreover, He wants His people to be brokers of that same culture. We are to grow so accustomed to the heavenly culture that we start to affect and infect everything and everyone around us with the look, values, style, vernacular, and feeling of heaven. In the process, we transform our homes, neighborhoods, cities, and nation by spreading the culture of heaven until it has gone viral, spreading into all the cultures of earth.

In the garden of Eden, the first man and woman, Adam and Eve, received a mandate from God to be fruitful, multiply, replenish, and subdue the earth. (See Genesis 1:28 KJV.) Why "replenish" and "subdue"? The dictionary defines *replenish* as "to make full or complete again, as by supplying what is lacking, used up, etc.,"[1] and *subdue* as "to overpower by superior force; overcome."[2] Why did God want Adam and Eve, our first parents, to do those things? My belief is that God wanted them to be responsible for continually spreading the culture of the garden of Eden into the undiscovered, unconquered parts of the world that had yet to experience the intimacy and fellowship with God that Adam and

1. replenish. Dictionary.com. *Dictionary.com Unabridged*. Random House, Inc. http://www.dictionary.com/browse/replenish (accessed: October 9, 2017).
2. subdue. Dictionary.com. *Dictionary.com Unabridged*. Random House, Inc. http://www.dictionary.com/browse/subdue (accessed: October 9, 2017).

Eve had been enjoying. The Father knew that every subsequent generation would have to be given a context for the initial garden-of-Eden experience, and Adam's job was to make sure this happened. He was to replenish the areas that had somehow lost Eden's culture, and he was to subdue the areas that had never experienced it before.

It is my conviction that God hasn't changed His mind about this task. The last Adam, Jesus Christ (see 1 Corinthians 15:45), has come and has tasked us with the same responsibility that was initially given to Adam and Eve. We are called to reflect the reality of heaven in our lives. Beyond that, we are called to spread the culture of heaven everywhere we go, causing a heavenly epidemic.

WE ARE CALLED TO REFLECT THE REALITY OF HEAVEN IN OUR LIVES. BEYOND THAT, WE ARE CALLED TO SPREAD THE CULTURE OF HEAVEN EVERYWHERE WE GO, CAUSING A HEAVENLY EPIDEMIC.

Early in ministry, I adopted an attitude that it was important to invest in the next generation. Even though I have just two natural children, it often felt as if I had ten children. I used to get so frustrated with all the kids always hanging out at our house. They ate all our food, broke all our furniture, stayed up all night, and never seemed to leave. It bothered me until I realized they hung around because they were attracted to the *culture* of our home. Most of these kids came from single-parent homes; they had never seen a family of people genuinely loving one another and working together. Many of them had grown up in homes where violence and/or substance abuse was the norm. Yet I watched their lives change as a result of their being exposed to the culture of heaven in my home. Those kids taught me a valuable lesson: When a culture has been established, people adapt to the norms within that culture.

> **THE CULTURE OF HEAVEN GOES WAY BEYOND DENOMINATION.... IT MAKES IT POSSIBLE FOR EVERY HUNGRY HEART TO ABIDE IN A CONTINUAL EXPERIENCE WITH A LIVING AND LOVING FATHER, REGARDLESS OF THEOLOGICAL BACKGROUNDS OR ARGUMENTS.**

This book is my small attempt to define some of the norms within the culture of heaven so that you might establish and then fortify them in your own lives. My prayer is that this book will awaken some of you to aspects of heaven's culture that have been unfamiliar to you. I hope to encourage others among you to press more deeply into parts of heaven's culture—parts that you may be experiencing in a superficial way at the moment. The culture of heaven goes way beyond denomination. It does what denominations can't do: It makes it possible for every hungry heart to abide in a continual experience with a living and loving Father, regardless of theological backgrounds or arguments.

I've heard it said, "A man with an experience is never at the mercy of a man with an argument, and a man with an argument is one experience away from having to change." Creating and releasing the culture of heaven places people on a collision course with the loving touch of God—a touch that changes lives forever.

God's Word says that we can experience heaven while on earth, and that the knowledge of His glory will cover the earth just as the waters cover the seas. (See Habakkuk 2:14.) When we allow the ideas, revelations, and ways of heaven to gain momentum in our lives, then earth's cultures are transformed by heaven's culture. When that happens, the promise given to the prophet Habakkuk will truly be fulfilled, and God's glory will be known in an experiential way in every nation under the sun.

1

MORE THAN YOU BARGAINED FOR

One thing I have learned in life is this: Hungry people see solutions where fattened people are blind.

When I was an impoverished college student in Washington, D.C., in the late eighties, I seemed to be perpetually hungry. Howard University is situated right in the middle of the city, and you had to become streetwise to survive. One of my survival strategies was to study in an all-you-can-eat restaurant. On certain days, a few friends and I would pack ourselves into a car and head to a place we'd found that provided a buffet. We'd pay the set price and then eat to our hearts' content. The goal was to eat all day for one low price. Once we had gorged ourselves, we'd break out the books and start studying at the table. Now, most young men have a superhuman capacity for putting food away; we were no exception, and in just over an hour, we'd all be hungry again. The books would be put away, and we'd head right back to the buffet. While I remember the restaurant management's not liking us too much, I also remember that no matter how much my friends and

I consumed, there was always more food than we could eat—even more than we could imagine eating.

What was true of my physical appetite, in time, became true of my spiritual hunger, as well. I began to cultivate the principle of "going for more"—that is, more of God's presence rather than more T-bone steaks and Maryland crabs. In 2006, this hunger led me to engage in a forty-day fast—something I'd learned you do when you're hungry for God, and something I had done five times prior. By then, I thought of myself as somewhat of an expert on the matter, but I later came to realize I didn't know a thing about fasting.

The truth is, I had learned the method but not the meaning of fasting. I had mastered the self-discipline of denying myself a plate, but I had failed to see what fasting was really all about. Up until then, I'd believed that the practice of fasting was meant to force God to do something for me. Thankfully, I began to see that fasting isn't a tactic designed to change God or twist His arm. Fasting is supposed to change us. It sure changed me. Fasting gave me a different perspective and heightened my awareness of God. It caused me to reorder my priorities, to become less consumed with trivial things.

During that time of consecration, I realized that fasting is about thanking God for what I already possess and hearing from Him about how to better steward my God-given possessions, not just asking Him for what I do not yet have. I saw that fasting is helpful as an expression of my hunger for anointings and breakthroughs I've yet to experience. At the same time, I knew I had to be careful not to believe that fasting would somehow "make" God give me something He was not ready to release. My heart needed to learn to be hungry and thankful at the same time. Often, people either fast in order to get something, only to end up disappointed by a lack of breakthrough, or they become so fixated on yesterday's breakthroughs that they build personal altars around those old breakthroughs and stop hungering for more of God.

Sooner or later, we have to understand that fasting is meant to be an outward sign of an inward longing, or an interior ache, for more of Him and Him alone.

WE HAVE TO UNDERSTAND THAT FASTING IS MEANT TO BE AN OUTWARD SIGN OF AN INWARD LONGING, OR AN INTERIOR ACHE, FOR MORE OF HIM AND HIM ALONE.

Fasting is a discipline that reflects our desire—the deepest desire of the human soul.

TAKE THE BLUE PILL

In the hit movie *The Matrix,* the wise leader Morpheus offers young Neo a choice: He can take either the red pill or the blue pill. Morpheus warns him that taking the blue pill will open his eyes and show him things as they truly are. The red pill will keep him in a dream world where he can remain in a sleepy oblivion.

Jesus is offering us the red pill or the blue pill. Religion is the red pill. By taking this pill, we deny ourselves true revelation and deprive ourselves of deep encounters with God as we settle for the dissatisfying routine of Christian tradition. The blue pill, on the other hand, produces an awakening. It leads us to open our hearts to the abundant, extraordinary life Jesus has promised us. It offers us a portal into the culture of heaven.

Through the practice of fasting and prayer, we get to explore this transcendent dimension of reality in a more profound way. When my fasting is motivated by the sheer joy of personal fellowship with God, that fellowship is only intensified, and I never end up disappointed because of what I did or didn't get from God. Time spent in His presence never leaves us depleted; it can only satisfy us more.

If you don't believe me, look at Jesus! After a long day of ministering to crowd after crowd of people, His disciples would go to sleep, while Jesus, on many occasions, would head to a quiet area to commune with His Father. Amazingly, the next morning, he never needed a nap; he never needed a day off. He was always energized and better equipped to do His Father's business.

Fellowship with God is the pinnacle and purpose of fasting. Along the way, we certainly receive other blessings, but God Himself is the great reward. If the only thing that a forty-day fast achieves is a time of deeper fellowship with God, then that fast was worth every hunger pang.

THE SUBTLE VOICE OF GOD

On the surface, my own forty-day fast didn't feel any different from the previous ones I had undertaken. However, this time, I received a revelation about my need for greater intimacy with the Father. When I concluded this particular fast, instead of experiencing the usual outcome, I saw God do something different.

I wish I could say I had a mind-blowing encounter with God. But one thing I've discovered is that mind-blowing encounters are the exception, not the rule, in forty-day fasts. More often than not, the Lord speaks so subtly that if you're not tuned in, His messages are easy to miss.

MORE OFTEN THAN NOT, THE LORD SPEAKS SO SUBTLY THAT IF YOU'RE NOT TUNED IN, HIS MESSAGES ARE EASY TO MISS.

When the prophet Elijah was on Mount Horeb, hiding from Queen Jezebel and her threats, the Lord spoke to him about his next assignment. His voice wasn't heard in the strong wind, the earthquake, or the fire; rather, it came on a gentle breeze. (See

1 Kings 19:1–18.) Elijah had to be tuned in enough to discern the difference, because, in times past, such natural elements as wind, earthquake, and fire had all signified God's presence. But not this time. This time, God communicated in a much subtler way.

It's often the subtle moves of God that are the most powerful. Maybe it's your perspective that's changed, or your desires that are taken to another level. It may seem insignificant, but these hard-to-detect changes probably mean loads more than you think.

In 2006, that's just what happened to me.

I had just graduated from seminary and was thinking about my life and what I would do next. At that time, everything pointed to my staying and serving in my home church. But then, a shift took place in me. I loved what we were doing at the church, but I suddenly became hungry to see more. I noticed that my prayers were changing. My preaching was changing. My overall outlook on ministry was changing. I found myself getting frustrated about what wasn't happening, even though what *was* happening was wonderful. In retrospect, I now realize that God had ignited a flame within me that set me longing for more of Him. Within two years, I left my home church and charted a course to do ministry differently, as an expression of what was burning in my heart.

STAYING HUNGRY WHEN YOU'RE FULL

I helped plant a church in Providence, Rhode Island, and I vividly remember that first year. Every day was like a new experience in God. It felt as if He was showing us new dimensions of His ways, moment by moment. We couldn't get enough of it. We were so desperate. At the time, we were intensely hungry for what we'd heard had happened in the revivals taking place in Toronto, Pasadena, Redding, and elsewhere. We wanted our ministry to look and feel like those churches, but we had no clue how to achieve that. So much of our hunger stemmed from our simply wanting answers to questions. In addition, a lot of our desperation had to do with the fact that we had no financial support. We were totally dependent on God for our provision. Our hunger for revival, need for finances, and excitement of starting a new ministry all combined to create a group of people who were hungry for God's presence.

After the first year, that church grew to a point where it could handle paying me a full-time salary. By the end of the second year and the beginning of the third, we were in negotiations for a new building. Walking into that building was a miracle in itself; going through the construction experience kept us desperate for God.

The period from 2006 to 2010 was marked by amazing passion and hunger, but as we entered 2011, I began to notice a shift taking place. Things had settled into a good pace for us. The church was growing, and our meetings always had evidence of the manifest presence of God. Enough miracles were happening to lead me to feel good about what we were doing. Our other ministries were doing well, too. However, our sense of desperation had waned.

I now had to deal with a more serious challenge than our financial situation or the strength of our burgeoning church. I had to figure out how to stay desperate when everything was going well. Up to this point, crises had motivated us to long for God. We cried out night and day for His presence when we didn't know where our next check was coming from or if people would show up on Sunday. God graciously responded to those pleas, but now we were faced with a greater crisis—the crisis of finding motivation in the midst of comfort.

KEEPING YOUR MOMENTUM

I've long been a student of Israel's history, and I've always been the guy who yelled at the Israelites when they experienced periods of great prosperity and peace, and forgot God in the process. The cycle seemed to be endless. Israel would encounter a major crisis and cry out to God for mercy. He would deliver them; they would prosper and forget God until the next crisis came along. Then they would cry out to God, and He would deliver them out of slavery and poverty to freedom and prosperity, all over again. The tragedy of this cycle, for Israel, is that it cost them progress. Several generations never traveled any farther than their forefathers; in some cases, a generation even regressed, ending up in a worse position than the previous generation. This cycle repeats itself again and again in the Old Testament.

When I found myself facing the same predicament, I stopped yelling in frustration at the Israelites. God had responded to our cries of desperation. He had established and prospered us. And I had forgotten God.

Two of my favorite Scripture passages are found in the book of Psalms and in 2 Corinthians. In effect, they both say the same thing:

> *How blessed is the man whose strength is in You, in whose heart are the highways to Zion! Passing through the valley of Baca they make it a spring; the early rain also covers it with blessings. They go from strength to strength, every one of them appears before God in Zion.* (Psalm 84:5–7)

> *But we all, with unveiled face, beholding as in a mirror the glory of the Lord, are being transformed into the same image from glory to glory, just as from the Lord, the Spirit.*
> (2 Corinthians 3:18)

In the verse from 2 Corinthians, I believe the apostle Paul was restating what the psalmist, in Psalm 84, described as a chief characteristic of the abundant spiritual life. We get better, stronger, and faster with each passing day. It was never the intention of God for His people to go backward and resign themselves to mediocre lives devoid of passion and purpose.

> **IT WAS NEVER THE INTENTION OF GOD FOR HIS PEOPLE TO GO BACKWARD AND RESIGN THEMSELVES TO MEDIOCRE LIVES DEVOID OF PASSION AND PURPOSE.**

After the death of Moses, his successor, Joshua, led the Israelites through a period of incredible expansion. They conquered every enemy nation standing in the way of their occupation of God's Promised Land. After forty years of warfare, expansion, and occupation, Caleb made this amazing statement to Joshua on Caleb's eighty-fifth birthday:

> *I am still as strong today as I was in the day Moses sent me; as my strength was then, so my strength is now, for war and for going out and coming in. Now then, give me this hill country about which the LORD spoke on that day....*
>
> (Joshua 14:11–12)

Caleb fought in wars for years but never arrived at a place of resignation. His declaration was that he was still ready to fight, for he was just as strong as when he'd first begun fighting.

OUR PRIESTLY CALLING

Oftentimes, people go through battles, achieve victories, build monuments to those victories, and camp out around those monuments. They stop progressing and spend the rest of their days living on yesterday's victory.

When Moses constructed the tabernacle, he was called by God to establish the priesthood as well. The priests were given a number of duties that had to do with ministering to the people and also to the Lord. One such duty was maintaining the fires that burned on the altar of sacrifice. The initial fire fell from God's presence, but it was the priest's responsibility to keep those fires burning all day, every day, so that God's manifest presence would never leave the community.

> *Command Aaron and his sons, saying, "This is the law for the burnt offering: the burnt offering itself shall remain on the hearth on the altar all night until the morning, and the fire on the altar is to be kept burning on it."* (Leviticus 6:9)

Jesus was the final sacrifice made to atone for the sin of man, which means that we no longer need physical altars. In addition, everyone who believes in Him has become a priest. (See 1 Peter 2:9; Revelation 1:6.) However, the responsibilities are the same: As God's new priests, we are tasked with keeping the fires burning, only these fires are now to burn on the altars of our hearts. Our personal hunger and our need for God's presence are meant to press us toward sacrificing whatever is required for us to keep the flame of God burning in our lives. Without our diligent attention, these flames falter. Indeed, this is precisely what happens to many believers. They remain positionally Christian, but they lose what it means to be passionately Christian. They learn the dysfunction of living apart from God's fire.

OUR PERSONAL HUNGER AND OUR NEED FOR GOD'S PRESENCE ARE MEANT TO PRESS US TOWARD SACRIFICING WHATEVER IS REQUIRED FOR US TO KEEP THE FLAME OF GOD BURNING IN OUR LIVES. WITHOUT OUR DILIGENT ATTENTION, THESE FLAMES FALTER.

Israel was never meant to know what it was to live without God's presence, but history tragically records that they found out. And the same fate easily befalls us, as well. During the time when I was witnessing the fruit of my spiritual hunger, I started to discover how the fire in our hearts can diminish slowly and almost imperceptibly. No Christian in his right mind ever consciously decides to walk away from his first love. But, over time, the distractions of life have a dousing effect on even the most devoted believers.

If we're not careful, a raging fire can slowly turn into a wisp of smoke.

THE DANGERS OF DISTRACTION

In life, we face two main categories of distraction: those that come from the enemy and those that arise from life itself.

The demonic distractions we face are those negative occurrences that appear out of nowhere and are designed by the enemy to frustrate our efforts to attain our God-given goals. They tend to surface most frequently when we're involved in something God has prompted us to do.

Once, I was en route to a very important reconciliation meeting with a friend in Columbus, Ohio. He and I hadn't spoken in several years following a conflict, and I knew it was time for us to work through our issues and reconcile. We both had ministry engagements in Columbus the same weekend, so we agreed to meet there. The morning of our meeting, I went to the airport, only to find that my plane had developed mechanical issues. I was taken off the flight and rerouted to another flight that ended up being delayed. It was then that I realized these were not just ordinary travel issues. Satan was trying to keep our meeting from happening.

My friend had a brief window of availability to meet. I needed to arrive in Columbus early enough to catch a cab to his hotel before he had to leave for his evening meeting. Once I realized what was happening in the spiritual realm, I immediately began praying and binding the work of the enemy. I knew God's heart was completely in favor of my reconciling with my friend, and so, based on that confidence, I declared that our meeting would happen.

Once my plane finally landed in Columbus, I went to the baggage claim and learned that my luggage hadn't made the flight. Filling out the necessary forms and going through the process of baggage retrieval took almost as much time as the flight itself, so I was really feeling the pinch. As soon as I got into a taxi, I called my friend and let him know I was finally on my way.

I stopped first at my hotel to check in, where I called my friend once more, to find out where he was staying so I could direct the cab driver accordingly. To my amazement, he was staying at the same hotel. I didn't have to catch another cab; I needed only take the elevator up one floor. As it turned out, the issues with my flight cost us only nominal time, and we had a glorious reconciliation—it was authentic and restorative. Our bond is stronger today than it was before our conflict took place.

THE ENEMY'S DIVERSIONS

> I believe that the greatest trick of the devil
> is not to get us into some sort of evil but
> rather have us wasting time.[3]
> —*Donald Miller*

Demonic distractions are intended to get us off task. In many cases, these distractions aren't evil on the surface. We deal with obvious evil tactics through prayer and through our declarations, but the less obvious distractions require a greater level of discernment. Avoiding such distractions may require us to sidestep certain individuals and activities.

When we started our church, a married couple joined our fellowship and brought with them some strange ideas. Because our congregation was still small, I was in the habit of making regular home visits at this point. I scheduled a visit with this new couple,

3. Donald Miller, *Blue Like Jazz* (Nashville, TN: Thomas Nelson, 2003), 13.

during which the wife shared with me a dream she'd had about me—a dream that caused her concern, because it didn't depict me in a very positive light.

> DEMONIC DISTRACTIONS ARE INTENDED TO GET US OFF TASK. IN MANY CASES, THESE DISTRACTIONS AREN'T EVIL ON THE SURFACE. WE DEAL WITH OBVIOUS EVIL TACTICS THROUGH PRAYER AND THROUGH OUR DECLARATIONS, BUT THE LESS OBVIOUS DISTRACTIONS REQUIRE A GREATER LEVEL OF DISCERNMENT.

One principle I've learned, in practicing the interpretation of our church members' dreams over the years, is that 99 percent of our dreams are not "messages" for other people but are rather a method God uses to communicate to us about ourselves. In the practice of interpreting dreams, I work with specific individuals to decipher what the people, places, and other details of their dreams mean for them.

I tried explaining this principle to the wife, but she remained absolutely convinced that there was something wrong with me, and that her dream was a God-given warning. For over an hour, I tried reasoning with her, to no avail. After several consecutive days of similar efforts on my part, the realization hit me over the head like an anvil: This woman was a demonic distraction in my life. I was spending entirely too much energy on e-mails, phone calls, and visits, trying to convince this woman and her husband of my integrity. It was then that I realized these two weren't going to change their minds. I lost three or four days of productivity because I was consumed with the troublesome and fallacious notions of one woman. On the surface, I was simply dealing with a church member's concerns—a responsibility of any good pastor. But it was more than that. This was a distraction that took me away from the work God had called me to do.

In the Old Testament, we read of Nehemiah, a godly man who led the effort to rebuild the wall of Jerusalem. Throughout his rebuilding project, Nehemiah was confronted by a number of men who continually opposed him and sought to sabotage his work. On one occasion, several of these men endeavored to have a conversation with Nehemiah, but he wisely decided to keep himself focused.

> *Now when it was reported to Sanballat, Tobiah, to Geshem the Arab and to the rest of our enemies that I had rebuilt the wall, and that no breach remained in it, although at that time I had not set up the doors in the gates, then Sanballat and Geshem sent a message to me, saying, "Come, let us meet together at Chephirim in the plain of Ono." But they were planning to harm me. So I sent messengers to them, saying, "I am doing a great work and I cannot come down. Why should the work stop while I leave it and come down to you?"*
>
> (Nehemiah 6:1–3)

Nehemiah didn't ignore these men; he dealt with them quickly and decisively, and he gave them no more of his time.

This is an abiding lesson: We shouldn't ignore demonic distractions, but neither should we dwell on them for longer than is necessary.

Remember this: The goal of demonic distractions is, in most cases, not to destroy us but to distract us. The enemy is trying to rob worthy tasks and causes of our attention.

In our church, we don't like talking about Satan except when it is absolutely necessary, because I've found people can become disproportionately devil-conscious and lose sight of the One we're supposed to gaze upon—that is, Jesus, the light of the world. It's not that we don't take the enemy seriously; we just live with an awareness that he is an inferior being, and we'd much rather give our energies toward fixating on the supremacy and goodness of God.

> THE GOAL OF DEMONIC DISTRACTIONS IS, IN MOST CASES, NOT TO DESTROY US BUT TO DISTRACT US. THE ENEMY IS TRYING TO ROB WORTHY TASKS AND CAUSES OF OUR ATTENTION.

In the face of demonic distractions, our discernment helps us to confront it quickly, get it behind us, and remain focused on what God has called us to do. That way, we keep moving forward as we keep the fires burning.

THE DISTRACTIONS OF LIFE

The distractions of life are quite simply those that arise as a result of our living on planet Earth.

Virtually all of these distractions have no evil source or intent whatsoever. In fact, ironically, many of these distractions are noble. Life's distractions are trickier to manage than demonic ones because they can often appear good. But, as the old saying goes, the good can distract us from the best.

In early 2014, I spent three weeks praying and fasting in South Korea. It had long been a desire of mine to observe an extended fast, and I knew I could never accomplish such a thing at home. I was bewildered because, at the time, I had completed six forty-day fasts, and I couldn't figure out why the seventh one was proving so difficult. I prayed about it, and the Lord simply said, "You're too distracted." I realized that I had undergone the previous fasts while serving as an associate pastor with limited responsibilities. Now, I had become a lead pastor of a growing congregation, with an entirely new, and far more extensive, set of demands consuming my time.

> **EVEN GOOD, WORTHWHILE TASKS CAN BECOME LIFE DISTRACTIONS THAT DIVERT US. WE MAY JUSTIFY THEM, SAYING THAT WE'RE DOING THEM IN THE NAME OF "MINISTRY," ALL THE WHILE FAILING TO DISCERN THAT THE GOOD IS DISTRACTING US FROM THE BEST.**

The distractions hindering me in this new season weren't demonic; they were the normal expectations of any senior pastor—"good" things, such as administrative tasks and speaking engagements. But, again, even good, worthwhile tasks can become life distractions that divert us. We may justify them, saying that we're doing them in the name of "ministry," all the while failing to discern that the good is distracting us from the best.

You may not be in the ministry at all. Maybe your biggest distractions have to do with the responsibilities of raising kids, completing projects at work, or helping out your friends or family members. You also may not have the luxury of being able to "leave it all behind" for three weeks, as I did. As a result, you're forced to implement a different strategy of carving out smaller pieces from your day or week for the exclusive purpose of seeking God's face. The point is that keeping the fires burning takes great effort and intentionality. We can't allow life's distractions, however good they may be, to divert us from the best thing of all—God's presence!

FINISHING WELL

> Faithful servants never retire. They serve faithfully as long as they are alive. You can retire from your career, but you will never retire from serving God.[4]
>
> —*Rick Warren*

4. Rick Warren, *The Purpose Driven Life* (Grand Rapids, MI: Zondervan, 2002), 262.

Most employed people always have, in the back of their mind, that glorious day when they will retire and take it easy for the rest of their lives. Every workday, they envision themselves sitting at home in their armchair, watching TV, or strolling across the well-manicured greens of their favorite golf course. Retirement is a goal that most people can't wait to reach. They imagine living in a sun-soaked haven with not a care in the world, enjoying the benefits of a pension plan designed to take care of their every financial need. American television is deluged with commercials showcasing companies ready to help people to plan and prepare for retirement.

In the kingdom of God, the longing for retirement can be a harmful thing. I'm not suggesting we work until we drop dead, but I am saying that believers should never lose their sense of purpose and destiny. As someone once put it, our task is not to become retired but "re-fired"!

King David entered into a season of retirement that diverted his attention away from his purpose in life and ended up causing him to fall into sin. When he decided to "sit one out" instead of leading his troops into battle, he found himself engrossed with Bathsheba and soon caught up in adultery. (See 2 Samuel 11.) In this case, "distraction" was an understatement, and it led to a massive moral failure—a failure whose origins lay in David's decision to take a breather from his God-given purpose.

Not all instances of retirement from kingdom work are as dramatic or as destructive as David's. But I have met many people who used to be "on fire" for God, only to level off and cruise casually to the finish line. We are not wired to coast home in this fashion. Constant advancement is always the best stance for the believer. The idea that Christians are supposed to throw in the towel and drop out of relevance at some point is a total myth. Our roles change, our demands change, but our purposes never do. Our hearts should beat with a passion to do what God has called us to do, even if we're in a season of handing the baton to the next runner, passing off part or all of the workload we used to carry. Any relay runner will tell you that he's running as hard as he can at the end of the race because he's aiming to keep his team in the lead, and because he has to catch up to the runner to whom he will hand the baton, who starts to run well before he receives said baton.

> **THE IDEA THAT CHRISTIANS ARE SUPPOSED TO THROW IN THE TOWEL AND DROP OUT OF RELEVANCE AT SOME POINT IS A TOTAL MYTH. OUR ROLES CHANGE, OUR DEMANDS CHANGE, BUT OUR PURPOSES NEVER DO.**

We have to keep running the race to the very end, even when we're passing the baton to someone else!

Church history and Scripture are replete with examples of people who started wonderfully but didn't finish well. King Solomon violated the one rule he was issued: "Don't marry foreign wives." In a spirit of haughtiness, and for the purpose of political alignments, he broke that rule and made decisions that would cost Israel for generations. When we pull back from our God-given assignment, we become vulnerable to competing interests. We lose the guiding compass of God's presence.

THE ENERGIZER BUNNY

At the beginning of 2008, I planted a church with ten other leaders, one of whom was Verna Brookins, a woman in her late sixties.

I had grown fond of Verna at our former church. She had joined after serving in a high position in the Church of God in Christ, and she sat in the congregation for eight years without telling anyone about her ministry pedigree. I finally learned of her background through a mutual friend, and I began having conversations with her.

I was amazed at Verna's wisdom and at the humility of her heart. Suffice it to say, we liked each other immediately. As time progressed, I brought her onto our leadership, and she served well. Our friendship continued to grow, and thus, when it was time to plant new ministries, I was ecstatic when she joined our team.

During one of our leadership meetings, I began to prophesy to her that God was going to cause her to do more in ministry over the next five years than she had done in her previous twenty-five years. She was excited about this word, and I was thrilled for her.

What I prophesied is exactly what has happened for Verna. I am awestruck at the vitality and productivity of this now seventy-four-year-old woman. She drives over ninety minutes one way to get to church every Sunday, and she conducts the Saturday meetings. I call her "the Energizer Bunny" because she just keeps going and going and going.

Verna Brookins has developed and trained prophetic teams, and has also created a school of prophecy that she takes to various places throughout the country. In her eighth decade of life, she's found her stride.

WE CAN'T ALLOW THE WORLD'S WAY OF THINKING TO DUPE US INTO RETIREMENT. WE HAVE BEEN BUILT TO BE RELEVANT FOR ALL OUR DAYS.

My point of sharing all this is that we can't allow the world's way of thinking to dupe us into retirement. We have been built to be relevant for all our days. The continual pursuit of God's presence, and the drive to fulfill His purpose for our lives, is what keeps our fires burning.

WELCOME TO THE BUFFET

I got far more than I had bargained for from that fast in 2006. In this book, I have attempted to share some of the secrets God has revealed to me about sustaining the personal and corporate revivals we long for. I'm no expert; I have to remind myself of these things constantly. But my humble prayer is that some of these secrets will be the key that starts the fire for you, or reignites the fire you've lost.

So, here we are. It isn't an all-you-can-eat joint; no, it's something better. It's a banquet the Father has prepared for us in the presence of our enemies.

We're invited to eat as much as we want; He just wants us to stay hungry.

Are you ready to receive more than you bargained for?

2

HARDWIRED FOR THE SUPERNATURAL

When you get close to God's face, the things that are found only in heaven start appearing on the earth.

While observing a fast in 2006, I learned many things. What was I after? The same thing you're after! I wanted more of God, more of His anointing—a greater measure, a fresh outpouring. I was tired of my so-called powerful Christian faith's being relegated to casting out a few devils or speaking in tongues in my prayer closet. I knew there was more. The Lord had told me to prophesy early on in my faith journey, and I tried to be very faithful to that word and gift. But even with my prophetic mantle, I felt there was more available. I just knew that there was more of heaven for me to access.

In reality, everyone is designed with a hunger for God. This craving was hardwired into Adam and Eve at creation when God gave them their threefold assignment: be fruitful, multiply, and subdue the earth. (See Genesis 1:28.) It was Adam and Eve's assignment to take the experience of the garden of Eden and extend it to the four corners of the earth. The freedom, peace, provision, dominion, and intimacy they enjoyed in Eden were to be established throughout the planet.

This demonstrates that Eden was much more than a geographic location; it was an atmospheric condition created by the presence of God and accessed by Adam and Eve through untainted faith. It was the original blueprint for the rest of the world.

It was the culture of heaven on earth.

> **WE ALL WERE BORN IN A STATE OF SEPARATION FROM GOD BECAUSE OF THE SINFUL ADAMIC NATURE RESIDING WITHIN US. BUT WHEN WE GET RIGHT WITH GOD...OUR FAITH IN CHRIST RECTIFIES THIS SYSTEMIC FAULT, AND JESUS GIVES US THE PASSWORD WITH WHICH WE CAN ACCESS HEAVEN.**

RUMORS OF EDEN

When a computer crashes, technical experts have the ability to retrieve the basic information stored on that computer by exploring its hard drive. Adam and Eve "crashed" and burned when they sinned, but the basic software package that had been hardwired into their system was preserved and now resides in every man and woman. Romans 5:12 tells us that when Adam sinned, all sinned. Adam's failure released something into the system of every person on the face of the earth; his sin infected the human software. Consequently, we all were born in a state of separation from God because of the sinful Adamic nature residing within us. But when we get right with God, by confessing our sins and repenting of them, our faith in Christ rectifies this systemic fault, and Jesus gives us the password with which we can access heaven.

As if that wasn't good enough, there's more.

We know that the Adamic virus has infected every person. One need look no further than the unspeakable atrocities perpetrated by mankind throughout the course of human history. But I also believe that the original software Adam received lies in every man and woman, just waiting for a repair and a reboot.

Let's consider an example.

Adam, the first man, was given the ability to name his world with his tongue. That ability has been passed down through every generation. Each human being, regardless of whether he is a follower of Christ, shares a common trait of a powerful tongue. That is why Proverbs 18:21 says, "*Death and life are in the power of the tongue.*" Even nonbelievers know about the power of positive speaking versus negative speaking. For believers, this power can be harnessed with greater sophistication and benefit.

A sin...consists in doing, saying, thinking,
or imagining anything that is not in perfect conformity
with the mind and law of God.[5]
—*J. C. Ryle*

Paul says in 1 Corinthians 2:16, "*We have the mind of Christ.*" As Christian believers, we have the thoughts and words of Christ available to us at all times. Our job is to come into agreement with Christ's mind and its contents. This agreement grants us access to a life of supernatural power such as Jesus led. The nonbeliever has not yet come into agreement with the mind of Christ, so his understanding of this power is more rudimentary. He is relegated to a reliance on his own positive thinking and the occasional encounter with the voice of God, which he may or may not recognize as such. Regardless, the power of the tongue is locked into the genetic code of every human being. In the same fashion, we all

5. J. C. Ryle, *Holiness* (Peabody, MA: Hendrickson Publishers, 2007), 19.

retain from Adam an internal longing to fulfill the task God originally assigned to us—to be fruitful, to multiply, and to subdue the earth.

Years ago, a medical doctor in our church conducted a study and found that when people perform feats of superhuman strength, they usually do so under great stress. She explained that under such conditions, the adrenal gland releases major doses of adrenaline, enabling these people to exhibit rare strength for such superhuman feats as lifting cars. Fear is the most common catalyst for this adrenal release. The doctor went on to explain that such high doses of adrenaline pose a real danger to the human body; we aren't designed to handle such strong fear-prompted releases on a consistent basis. She said, "We're not wired for fear."

The doctor was right, of course. Yet I believe we are wired to have the superhuman—or the supernatural—operating in our lives. The difference is that fear is no longer the motivator. Instead, our driving force becomes an inner desire to fulfill the Father's assignment.

What happened to me during that period of fasting in 2006 was that God rebooted my software and began to show me what it could really do.

A SUPERNATURAL GENERATION

Today, a generation is emerging that will fully grasp its rightful inheritance and start invading the culture with creative power, signs, and wonders. This generation is unusually hungry for the supernatural.

I don't know if you've noticed, but there's been a surge of interest in the supernatural. There are more books and movies today about vampires, superheroes, witches, and other types of super-charged humans than ever before. While I can understand why this fact concerns some people, I am personally excited by it. Even if the beings depicted are mostly misguided, counterfeit expressions of the supernatural, at their core, they are evidence of the unique wiring God has placed in every human—a longing for the supernatural.

In all of creation, humans are the only species that God said He made in His image. (See Genesis 1:26.) He wasn't just talking about outward appearances. He was actually saying that His DNA—His software—had been downloaded into human beings. From that identity, Adam and Eve began to demonstrate a likeness to God that was surpassed only in the Person of Jesus Christ. Jesus was at the same time fully God and fully man. Every miracle He performed, He performed simply as a man in right relationship with God. It's staggering to realize that Jesus told us we would not only perform the same types of miracles He did but would even go further in the supernatural than He did. (See John 14:12.) What an astonishing responsibility we carry.

LONGING FOR SPIRITUAL POWER

> God has privileged us in Christ Jesus to live above the ordinary human plane of life. Those who want to be ordinary and live on a lower plane can do so, but as for me, I will not.[6]
>
> —*Smith Wigglesworth*

One of the great tragedies of Christianity in the Western world is that we've learned to analyze Scripture, but we don't experience scriptural realities firsthand. We have become a people who glorify mental assent and demonize real encounters. Society has forced us to ignore our natural instincts. Our logical way of thinking keeps us from fulfilling our God-given responsibility.

---

6. Smith Wigglesworth, *Smith Wigglesworth on Spirit-Filled Living* (New Kensington, PA: Whitaker House, 1998), 16.

And yet, evidence of our supernatural and superhuman capacities keeps surfacing. Iris Global, a Christian humanitarian organization started by missionary Heidi Baker, stopped counting how many people they had raised from the dead once they surpassed 100. Randy Clark, founder of Global Awakening, gives testimonies almost daily about surgically implanted metal in people's bodies miraculously ceasing to restrict movement. Bethel Church in Redding, California, under the leadership of Bill Johnson, sends teams of evangelists into the city on a weekly basis, returning wonderful stories of miracles and breakthrough.

At the same time, the increase of stories about counterfeit supernatural beings is really a hidden cry for an experience that is authentic. I believe the time is ripe. First Corinthians 4:20 says that the kingdom of God is not a matter of talk but of power. God is raising a generation of people who have decided to reclaim their God-given responsibility and respond to the thirst in humankind for an encounter with the supernatural power of God. These people have said, "No more words; let me just show you what I am wired to do." This is the generation of people who are into movies about vampires, witches, and superheroes. They laugh because, deep down, they already sense that the feats depicted in Hollywood films will be mere child's play compared to the real supernatural encounters they are going to have when the culture of heaven invades earth.

GOD IS RAISING A GENERATION OF PEOPLE WHO HAVE DECIDED TO RECLAIM THEIR GOD-GIVEN RESPONSIBILITY AND RESPOND TO THE THIRST IN HUMANKIND FOR AN ENCOUNTER WITH THE SUPERNATURAL POWER OF GOD. THESE PEOPLE HAVE SAID, "NO MORE WORDS; LET ME JUST SHOW YOU WHAT I AM WIRED TO DO."

MISSION: IMPOSSIBLE

I am a complete spy-movie nut. From *Mission: Impossible* to James Bond to the Jason Bourne series, it's my favorite genre of film. I think it's the spy's isolation that most appeals to me. The hero always finds himself having to fulfill an assignment that will save his nation or the entire planet, all while overcoming seemingly insurmountable odds in distant and dangerous lands, where he's completely cut off from any support. The only things the spy can rely on are his training and his gadgets.

As a pastor, I sometimes feel as if I'm Ethan Hunt, being sent on a seemingly impossible mission. The difference is, I'm not doing it for a temporary group of national leaders; I'm serving a government that has no end to its increase. I'm also not alone, for God is with me, and He has more than just earthly gadgets to help me in my mission. He has supernatural signs, wonders, and miracles—the power of heaven.

When we think about the assignment our heavenly Father has given us, it may seem like an impossible mission. Indeed, the odds are incredibly great. But we also know that greater is He who is in us than he who is in the world. (See 1 John 4:4.) The task becomes impossible only if we try to accomplish it through our own strength. But when we remember what, and who, is in us, the odds don't seem insurmountable at all.

Think back to Adam's original instructions from God: be fruitful, multiply, and subdue the earth. He was charged with going throughout the earth and distributing the goodness of God in order to remove chaos and supplant disorder—an impossible mission, to the naked eye; but Adam was walking in complete intimacy with the Father, so he didn't see any difficulty at all, only opportunities.

Of course, when Adam fell into sin, his intimacy with the Father was broken, and he became aware of both his isolation and the size of the challenge set before him. His carnal eyes were opened to see problems that had previously been invisible to him. At the same time, however, the fullness of God's plan began to unfold. In Genesis 3:15, we are given a prophetic picture of Jesus crushing Satan. In fulfillment of this Scripture, Jesus later defeated Satan at Calvary and took back the authority over the earth that Adam had abdicated. In Matthew 28:18, He says, *"All authority has been given to Me in heaven and on earth."*

JESUS'S VICTORY, IN AND OF ITSELF, IS IMPRESSIVE AND WORTHY OF PRAISE, BUT HE DIDN'T STOP THERE. HE PASSED THE BATON AND RELEASED HIS AUTHORITY INTO THE HANDS OF EVERY BELIEVER.

Jesus's victory, in and of itself, is impressive and worthy of praise, but He didn't stop there. He passed the baton and released His authority into the hands of every believer. In fact, He commanded all believers to take up the baton and continue the assignment He was sent to do, saying, *"As the Father has sent Me, I also send you"* (John 20:21). What was Jesus sent to do? We find the answer in 1 John 3:8: *"The Son of God appeared for this purpose, to destroy the works of the devil."* We are sent to identify the works of Satan and then supplant them with heaven's reality. This means that the cross of Christ was the atonement and the assignment at the same time. Jesus purchased our salvation and put us back to work to complete Adam's unfinished business.

Whenever we see sickness, disease, and heartache, we are to identify those things as works of Satan and then release God's kingdom into the situation, thereby overthrowing whatever strongholds the enemy has attempted to set up. Tragically, so much of our modern theological thought does not allow for this process. Well-meaning Christians have developed a belief system in which no one expects any miracles to occur, because it's easier to expect nothing supernatural than it is to take the risk of believing God for the impossible.

This is not the way things were meant to be. When we fully give ourselves to the anointing of God, all things become possible for those who believe. (See Matthew 19:26; Mark 9:23; 10:27.) As Jesus said, *"If you have faith and do not doubt,...even if you say to this mountain, 'Be taken up and cast into the sea,' it will happen"* (Matthew 21:21). We are able to speak to the mountains of poverty and despair and see them cast into the sea. The impossible mission becomes possible on a regular basis. We start to witness seemingly hopeless situations bow down and submit to God's kingdom realities.

HEAVEN ON THE STREETS

After my 2006 fast, I noticed I had become bolder in my willingness to share my faith. This time it was different, however; I didn't just want to talk with people about the Gospel. I was hungry to demonstrate God's power.

At the outset of our ministry, our church went on a "treasure hunt"—a form of evangelism that was first introduced to the body of Christ by Kevin Dedmon. Kevin wrote a book about this type of evangelism called *The Ultimate Treasure Hunt: Digging for God's Treasure*. I've made it required reading in our church. Kevin, a leader at Bethel Church in Redding, California, is a skilled communicator. He teaches that in a "treasure hunt," teams of people come together for brief prayer to receive words of knowledge, or "clues," for their hunt. The team members share their clues with one another and then, based on those clues, go searching for the "treasure"—people whom God has specifically selected for an encounter with Him.

On the day of our hunt, I went out with a team of four. One of the young men in my group, Rob, had clues on his map about an African-American man on a bike in downtown Providence. Another clue indicated that the man needed prayer for his arm.

When we went to an area fitting the description provided by a clue from another team member's map, there he was—an African-American man sitting on his bike in the center of downtown Providence, just as Rob had seen in prayer! Excited, Rob bolted across the street to speak to the gentleman. The rest of us followed him and soon introduced ourselves. We explained to the man what we were doing, and then we asked if we could pray for any physical conditions that might be troubling him.

He looked at us. "Sure," he said. "Would you pray for my left arm? My bicep exploded in a weight-lifting accident."

Even more faith began to rise in us.

When he showed us his left arm, we could clearly see there had been a serious rupture in his bicep; the muscle did not assume the normal shape when he flexed it. The appearance was that of a balloon that had lost all its air.

Rob and I laid hands on the man and began to command life back into the arm. Suddenly, beads of sweat started forming on the man's left arm. To our amazement, as sweat poured from his arm, his bicep started to grow back to its normal size, right in front of our eyes. The other members of our team gathered around, and none of us could stop praising our God.

I asked the gentleman how he was feeling.

"My arm is incredibly hot," he replied.

The man must have received a jolt of faith himself, because he abruptly jumped off his bike and lifted it with his left arm, then looked at us with an expression of astonishment. "I can't do this!" he cried. "I can't do this!"

"You look pretty good," I replied. "Why don't you just go ahead and get a workout?"

The man started doing a set of bicep curls with his left arm—the arm that God had just healed.

A friend of his had been watching all this unfold. As we started to leave, she grabbed the young lady in our group, Cheryl, and asked her to pray that God would deliver her from an addiction to cigarettes. Cheryl laid hands on the woman and prayed. We watched as the glory of God fell upon this woman as well.

It was a wonderful day, watching heaven invade downtown Providence. This was exactly what I had been hungering for. I was longing for these types of encounters to be a normal part of my Christian experience. The government we serve has no end, and it's a kingdom of peace. Our Leader has put you and me on assignment to save the planet. We're fully equipped to fulfill our task because He is in the field with us. It is not an impossible mission, for we carry an anointing that is stronger than any obstacle we may face.

HUNGRY FOR THE ANOINTING

> Fasting is what prepares you for a new anointing.[7]
> —*Jentezen Franklin*

One of the great by-products of the time I spent fasting before the Lord was that, unknown to me until later, He had given me more of His own anointing. God's anointing had been something I simply didn't understand how to access, as much as I certainly coveted it. I would hear about supernatural moves of God in faraway lands, and would dream about being a part of them. During one season, I was so hungry for spiritual increase that I started making plans to shut down my ministry in the United States so I could move my family to Zimbabwe and join a ministry that was experiencing the things I had heard about. Hunger for more of

7. Jentezen Franklin, *Fasting* (Lake Mary, FL: Charisma House, 2007), 49.

God started to drive me. I knew that if I was ever to see the kinds of miracles I had heard and read about, I would need "more, Lord!" I would need more of His anointing.

You may be asking, "What do you mean by 'the anointing'?"

In the Old Testament, the anointing is a symbol of ordination into the office of priest, prophet, or king. It represents the power of God endowing a person. The high-quality olive oil used in the anointing came from olives that had been beaten and then hung in baskets so that the oil would drip through the fissures. Later in this book, we'll talk about the "beatings" we must endure if we desire to have the anointing refined in our lives.

The designation of Christ is a translation of the Greek word *Christos*, which means "anointed." Thus, "Christ" means literally "the anointed One." In the gospel of Luke, Jesus explained that He was able to do His ministry because the Spirit of the Lord had anointed Him for the work. (See Luke 4:18.)

When I was a child, I viewed Jesus as a type of Superman. Based upon what I was taught, I believed He was someone to be admired from afar, not someone to emulate. As I grew older, I realized that Jesus's earthly life has set for us a pattern to follow. Although Jesus was the Son of God, He was also fully human, born supernaturally of a virgin, and thus depended on the Holy Spirit's anointing to fulfill the mandate of His Father. In John 5:19, Jesus said, "*The Son can do nothing of Himself, unless it is something He sees the Father doing; for whatever the Father does, these things the Son also does in like manner.*" Later on, He said that He was restricted to speaking only what His Father spoke. (See John 12:49.) Jesus was a servant, of mankind and of His Father. It says in Philippians 2:6–7 that Jesus, though equal with God, did not cling to that status but rather emptied Himself of all deity and became a servant.

JESUS PERFORMED MIRACLES AND MINISTERED TO PEOPLE AS A MAN, COMPLETELY RELIANT UPON THE HOLY SPIRIT'S ANOINTING. IT IS THAT SAME ANOINTING THAT RAISED YOU AND ME FROM SPIRITUAL DEATH AND NOW LIVES IN US, EMPOWERING US TO PARTICIPATE IN GOD'S MINISTRY JUST AS JESUS DID.

One of the great cornerstones of the Christian faith is the fact that Jesus was fully God and fully man at the same time. During His earthly life, Jesus performed miracles and ministered to people as a man, completely reliant upon the Holy Spirit's anointing. It is that same anointing that raised you and me from spiritual death and now lives in us, empowering us to participate in God's ministry just as Jesus did. Jesus knew, from firsthand experience, how important the anointing was, such that He warned His disciples not to do anything until they had received this type of outpouring from God. (See Luke 24:49; Acts 1:4–5.) These disciples had seen more miracles than Elijah and Elisha combined; they had participated in the most impressive ministry in all history, and yet that pedigree was not nearly enough for the task ahead of them. Even with all their experience and past exploits, they still needed an increased measure of anointing.

DRAMA WITHOUT POWER

Without the anointing of God's Holy Spirit, ministry is reduced to performances aimed at outdoing the performances of others, prompting a vicious cycle of one-upmanship that seduces well-meaning ministries into adopting Hollywood standards and practices. The chase for God then gets replaced with striving for a bigger and better show. Pastors rely on dramatic effects to whip themselves and others into frenzies when they should simply rely on the purity of God's authentic power. We should never employ dramatic effect as a substitute for genuine encounters.

> **WITHOUT THE ANOINTING OF GOD'S HOLY SPIRIT, MINISTRY IS REDUCED TO PERFORMANCES AIMED AT OUTDOING THE PERFORMANCES OF OTHERS, PROMPTING A VICIOUS CYCLE OF ONE-UPMANSHIP THAT SEDUCES WELL-MEANING MINISTRIES INTO ADOPTING HOLLYWOOD STANDARDS AND PRACTICES.**

The quest for drama instead of power sometimes spills over into our worship. Don't get me wrong; I love vibrant worship experiences in which everybody—musicians, singers, sound technicians, thespians, dancers, and more—brings their best to the table and celebrates our God. Extravagant worship is what we were made for, and it is certainly a core value of the church. But I've experienced worship in settings of expensive stage designs, high-tech smoke machines, fancy lights, great acoustics…and no anointing. These types of meetings leave you with a feeling that it was great going down, but now there's an indigestion you just can't shake. When Madison-Avenue marketing has replaced the anointing, something is seriously wrong.

One of my responsibilities at a church I used to work with was training the worship team to invoke the presence of God. I routinely reminded them not to depend on good lighting and smoke machines, because we were starting to have such glorious worship experiences that God's glory was actually releasing its own visible haze in the building. I didn't want anyone to mistake the genuine signs and wonders that had visited our church as something we created through a machine.

Showman P. T. Barnum, of circus fame, is quoted as having said, "There's a sucker born every minute." Barnum took advantage of people's gullibility and made a profit selling bogus items to those frustrated with life and longing for any chance to escape day-to-day reality. But God isn't looking for "suckers." The church owes the world an authentic encounter with the only living God.

In Exodus 33, Moses prayed to the Lord, saying, "If Your presence does not go with us, what else will distinguish us from all the other people on the face of the earth?" (See verses 15–16.) Moses understood that it is God's power that makes us different from any other social organization on the planet. It's the presence of God that forms the unique identity marker of the people of God. For us Christians, only the anointing really sets us apart.

MISSIONS WITH MIRACLES

We modern people think of miracles as
the suspension of the natural order,
but Jesus meant them to be the restoration of
the natural order. The Bible tells us that
God did not originally make the world to have disease,
hunger, and death in it. Jesus has come to redeem where
it is wrong and heal the world where it is broken. His
miracles are not just proofs that he has
power but also wonderful foretastes of
what he is going to do with that power.[8]
—*Tim Keller*

Let's face it: There are groups that do a much better job of meeting certain socioeconomic needs than many churches. We have to be honest about that. However, there is something unique that only the church can bring to the table, and that's the anointing—the supernatural, heavenly power to change seemingly impossible situations in people's lives. No other organization on the planet can do that!

It has been a privilege of mine to help send missionaries to foreign nations with food, clothing, and medical supplies, but

8. Timothy J. Keller, *The Reason for God* (New York: Penguin Books, 2008), 95–96.

the base necessity that every missionary must carry is the power of God. More than simply distributing food and supplies, these missionaries also mend broken marriages, heal broken bodies, and drive out demons from people. Now, with the emergence of the millennial generation, we have an even greater opportunity to partner the power of God with a keen sense of social justice and a strong desire to heal geopolitical concerns.

> **THERE IS SOMETHING UNIQUE THAT ONLY THE CHURCH CAN BRING TO THE TABLE, AND THAT'S THE ANOINTING—THE SUPERNATURAL, HEAVENLY POWER TO CHANGE SEEMINGLY IMPOSSIBLE SITUATIONS IN PEOPLE'S LIVES. NO OTHER ORGANIZATION ON THE PLANET CAN DO THAT!**

This is the unique element we have to offer—the power of heaven operating here on earth.

The leaders of YWAM (Youth With A Mission) Boston, Doug and Debi Tunney, are wonderful friends of mine with a heart for activating young people into evangelism. Over dinner one evening, Doug told me about a recent trip the couple had taken to a village in Liberia. Their goal was to preach the gospel there; by all accounts, they succeeded, and people came to Christ. But Doug had noticed that the women in the village all wore similar bracelets around their wrists. He later found out that these were not just bracelets but amulets they had been given for the purpose of warding off a curse the village witch doctor had placed on the children. The locals took this curse very seriously. Several babies had died of mysterious causes, and most people attributed their deaths to the witch doctor's curse.

Doug said he knew that if this village was going to experience any real breakthrough, this demonic spirit would need to be dealt with. One day, he felt a surge of faith to challenge the mothers to take off their bracelets, renounce the curse, and give their hearts to Jesus. He explained to them that no power was greater than the power of God. They listened but were still not convinced. In many African cultures, supernatural power is not viewed with the same sense of astonishment as most Westerners view it. There is a respect for, and a familiarity with, spiritual power that most Westerners just don't understand. The supernatural, including the concepts of witch doctors and spells, is treated more seriously.

As Doug was exhorting the villagers, the witch doctor entered the church building and started taunting him. Acting in faith, Doug commanded the evil spirit to leave the witch doctor. He then watched as the man fell to the ground in a heap. After several minutes, Doug approached the man and began ministering to him. Soon the man rose to his feet, faced Doug, and told him that he wanted to be a follower of Jesus Christ. Doug prayed with him and led him to Christ. The entire village was freed from their fear of the former witch doctor. One by one, the mothers took off their bracelets and gave their hearts to Jesus. Once again, Christ's kingdom had come and dispelled the darkness. It was the power of God that made the difference.

AN IRRESISTIBLE GOODNESS

It is the anointing that enables us to see God's kingdom come and His will being done on earth as in heaven.

When Moses asked God to show him His glory, God responded by revealing His goodness. (See Exodus 33:18–19.) What an incredible revelation! God's glory is full of goodness. And God's anointing is designed to bring His unrelenting, world-changing goodness to earth.

There are spiritually hungry people who don't want any more rhetoric, politics, or other routine schemes; they are simply hungering for an authentic encounter with God. They want to experience His goodness firsthand.

Right now, the United States is in the middle of a cultural war. Lines have been drawn in the sand about this position and that principle. However, I believe that when people see the goodness of God, it will render all political and cultural issues irrelevant. God's power will inform conversations in such a way that people will develop policies and take positions that reflect the nature of God and consequently prompt a deeper longing for encounters with God's kindness that will draw others into relationship with Him.

It's time to return to the original mandate of Eden.

The software that was built into each one of us at creation is designed to make us function like our Father.

By design, therefore, we can lead others, by our words and our deeds, into encounters with God's irresistible goodness.

When that happens, the culture of heaven will invade, and the cultures of this earth will be completely transformed.

3

PAYING FOR YOUR OIL

God has a way of giving us what we ask for, but in ways we never seem to anticipate, and sometimes in ways we have to be sensitive enough to recognize. The anointing that I longed for did increase in my life, but it didn't come according to the way I had envisioned.

In Matthew 25:1–10, Jesus described the kingdom of heaven by telling a story about ten virgins awaiting the arrival of their bridegroom. You probably know how it pans out: Five of the virgins were wise; the other five were unwise. The five wise virgins were willing to pay a price for the oil needed to keep their lamps lit. The other five were considered unwise because, instead of paying for their own oil, they attempted to benefit from the oil that the other virgins had bought.

I am an absolute believer in spiritual inheritances. In my life and ministry, I have a keen awareness that I am riding a wave of momentum for which many spiritual fathers and mothers in my life paid a heavy price. However, I cannot allow myself to simply rest on the momentum of my forebears. I have to pay my own price to increase that which God did in me through the influence of others.

Ours is one of the most technologically advanced generations the planet Earth has ever seen. We have developed countless conveniences, ways of providing instant gratification. But the drawback is that many people don't appreciate the effort that is needed for greater, spiritual rewards. They don't realize that there is a price to pay in order to experience breakthrough. Many believers say to themselves, "If I can just get this person to lay hands on me," or "If I can just get to this conference, then my problem will fade in an instant." While instantaneous miracles can and do happen, God wants to see each new generation willing to pay for its own oil.

THE OIL COMES FROM PRESSING

> Character cannot be developed in ease and quiet.
> Only through experience of trial and suffering
> can the soul be strengthened, ambition inspired,
> and success achieved.[9]
> —*Helen Keller*

Acts 14:22 says, "*Through many tribulations we must enter the kingdom of God.*" In all honesty, much of my own anointing has come from experiences of great tribulation. Personal or corporate tribulation is not a popular subject, especially in a kingdom that is so full of joy, where the King is known to be always good. However, the reality is that in this fallen world of ours, we are bound to encounter many difficulties and confront constant challenges. We are forced to embrace the tension of knowing how good God is while we endure harrowing trials, and to resolutely refuse to bow the knee to depression, oppression, and unbelief. Managing this tension well is a sign of spiritual maturity and opens a gateway to greater power in God.

---

9. Helen Keller, *Hellen Keller's Journal 1936–1937* (New York: Doubleday, Doran & Company, Inc., 1938), 60.

WE ARE FORCED TO EMBRACE THE TENSION OF KNOWING HOW GOOD GOD IS WHILE WE ENDURE HARROWING TRIALS, AND TO RESOLUTELY REFUSE TO BOW THE KNEE TO DEPRESSION, OPPRESSION, AND UNBELIEF. MANAGING THIS TENSION WELL IS A SIGN OF SPIRITUAL MATURITY AND OPENS A GATEWAY TO GREATER POWER IN GOD.

For many people, the tension caused by living with a loving God while facing intense tests is too problematic, prompting them to create cheap theology that attempts to resolve the difficulty. Such a response is spiritually dysfunctional, because all man-made answers violate the nature of God's goodness. Believers cannot afford to compromise biblical truth and settle for a lesser reality of God. Speaking for myself, I will not embrace the false, unscriptural notion that Father God sends problems my way in order to teach me a lesson or to strengthen my faith. No, I will stand on the biblical belief that God will use the difficulties in my life to draw me into a deeper relationship with Him.

Here, we must distinguish between God's decretive will and His permissive will. I do not believe that God, as a good Father, decrees that I should suffer. But I do believe He sometimes permits me to suffer so that I might grow as His son. He is a loving Father who turns everything to good because He is good. (See Romans 8:28.)

Let's explore this concept at a more down-to-earth level. I certainly would never imagine inflicting one of my own children with a life-threatening disease because I felt he needed to work on his humility, or another virtue. What kind of a father would that make me? It is crazy to think that our Father in glory would do such a thing to His kids, yet there are many in the church today who reason their way to such a conclusion in an effort to explain to people why they are going through the difficulties they're facing.

I refuse to subscribe to this substandard line of thought. Even though we believers are not of this world, we live in the world—a world that is fallen and in need of redemption. Therefore, many of our greatest challenges are simply the result of our living on a planet that is still groaning for its liberation, still aching for full redemption. (See Romans 8:22–23.) The Father allows us to experience suffering, but He gives us grace not only to endure but also to be strengthened in our inner man. The result is increase for us.

HOT-WATER MOMENTS

One key to increasing the measure of our anointing is realizing, first of all, that there is a cost for that anointing; and, second, that each person must pay for his or her own oil. Living wisely in the tension between the mystery of God's limitless kindness and the extreme challenges of life can trigger a fresh outpouring of His anointing.

Consider again Jesus's parable of the ten virgins in Matthew 25:1–10. In the story, as the virgins awaited their bridegroom, the five who had not purchased their own oil wanted to borrow oil from the five who had come prepared, having already purchased their own oil. However, the "unwise virgins" weren't allowed to borrow oil; they had to go and purchase their own, and, in so doing, they missed the arrival of the bridegroom.

There are moments when Christ, our heavenly Bridegroom, shows up wanting to do something in us or for us, and we find ourselves lacking the necessary oil. We may be able to get in on someone else's anointing for a season, but, sooner or later, there comes a time when we will have to provide our own oil if we desire to participate in what God is doing.

> **WE MAY BE ABLE TO GET IN ON SOMEONE ELSE'S ANOINTING FOR A SEASON, BUT, SOONER OR LATER, THERE COMES A TIME WHEN WE WILL HAVE TO PROVIDE OUR OWN OIL IF WE DESIRE TO PARTICIPATE IN WHAT GOD IS DOING.**

I've heard it said, "The anointing is free, but it isn't cheap." Often, people want more of God's anointing, but they don't want to pay the price for it. The path to accessing greater measures of power involves learning to manage tests and tribulations well.

A friend of mine had this as his favorite saying: "If you want to know what's inside of a tea bag, you put it in hot water." "Hot water"—times of trial and difficulty—present us with a critical opportunity in our walk with God. When we're in hot water, we have a chance to be transformed from the inside out. God's expectation is that we will be willing to go through the "hot water" moments and pay the price in order to carry an anointing that makes us ready for when He shows up.

TWO TURBULENT YEARS

After my fast, I entered a period that was tumultuous, to say the least. I began experiencing a virtual fog in my Christian life.

At the time, I was an associate pastor in a vibrant church, with increasing opportunities to minister. But I couldn't shake the feeling that there was something more. I studied harder, worked harder, and ministered harder, trying to initiate the "more" on my own.

My influence was increasing, and my salary was growing—certainly, this was the way "more" looked in my imagination. Yet, every so often, God would disturb my complacency with a nagging question: "Son, if I took all of this away, would you trust Me?"

I have to admit, things were going so well at the time, I initially thought it was the devil tormenting me. Within a few months, things really began to unravel. The year that had started with such promise proved to be the beginning of two years of the worst tumult I have ever experienced. In the end, I left the church I had served for fifteen years.

Those two years proved to be the most challenging season of my life. At the same time, my burning passion to see more of God kept increasing.

Charles Dickens's *A Tale of Two Cities* opens with the iconic line "It was the best of times, it was the worst of times." Looking back, that phrase aptly sums up the season I was in. It was the worst time of my life, in terms of trials, and yet my hunger for more of God was ablaze in a way it had never been before. Thus, it was also the best of times.

MORE OF YOU, LORD

> If you aren't hungry for God, you are full of yourself.
> That's why God cannot fill you with His Spirit.
> But if you will empty yourself, if you will die to self, you'll
> be a different person by the time you
> reach the last page of this book.[10]
> —*Mark Batterson*

Sensing such intense spiritual hunger, I began to fast and pray in order to discern the city in which God would have me minister next. Some well-meaning people thought I should take a year off and do nothing besides heal and reflect on "the meaning of life." What they didn't understand was that I was actually more excited about ministry than I had ever been before. It was as if God was blowing a fresh wind over my life. I received some

10. Mark Batterson, *All In* (Grand Rapids, MI: Zondervan, 2013), 21.

helpful Christian counseling on the heels of the setback, but, honestly, my time with God is what made the most significant impact. I have wonderful, close friends who are psychologists, and they are excellent at what they do; I deeply respect their ministry in the kingdom. In my estimation, any relevant ministry must include a genuine commitment to mental health. I place a high value on holistic healing and counseling. But at that time in my life, I just wanted God.

During this season, the thought of introspection and self-reflection was nauseating. I actually became sick of telling well-wishers who called to check on me "I am okay!" I was just hungry to go and do what the Lord had been showing me in visions and dreams. This newfound hunger for ministry wasn't a Band-Aid to mask the pain inside. No, it was born out of the infilling I had been experiencing in the secret places in God.

It was a tough call to say good-bye to the people I had loved so intensely for so long, and to part under such negative circumstances. At the same time, I found myself singing songs of joy given uniquely to me by God. I started having the most intimate encounters with God that I have ever known. His manifest presence became more tangible, and I was learning how to encourage myself in the Lord.

I have since reconnected with many of the people I had to say good-bye to, and God has ushered me into a series of joyful reconciliations with them. It is said that people are defined by what they do in times of crisis, and the grace and humility these individuals brought to our reconciliations gave me an even greater respect for them than I had originally had. Looking back, I now realize that this period of time wasn't about them; it was about paying for my oil. This oil, I've come to understand, has greater significance. What I wanted for the purpose of ministry needed first to be ministered to me.

DEEP CALLS TO DEEP

One of the most important lessons I learned in my time of great tribulation is how much more interested the Father is in me, as a person, than in anything He could give me. He could have delivered me from my sorrows in the blink of an eye, but He wanted to redeem my time of trouble for the sake of who I am. As a result, I now stand with a fresh anointing over my identity (who I am) and my ministry (what I do).

ONE OF THE MOST IMPORTANT LESSONS I LEARNED IN MY TIME OF GREAT TRIBULATION IS HOW MUCH MORE INTERESTED THE FATHER IS IN ME, AS A PERSON, THAN IN ANYTHING HE COULD GIVE ME.

Psalm 42 is the cry of a man in a time of great tribulation. In the midst of his troubles, he remembers God, and his heart calls out to the Lord for help. The psalmist describes this anguished prayer as "deep calling out to deep." (See Psalm 42:7.)

I can identify with the psalmist, because, in the midst of all the pressure I was under, the depths of my heart kept calling out to God to be in harmony with His Spirit, for Him to intervene for me.

Something unique happens when the depth of our spirit cries out to the depth of God's. There's an exchange, of sorts, that occurs. We come to the Father, crying in anguish, and the Lord responds with healing and revelation from a deep reservoir that never runs dry.

This reservoir—the deep places in God—contains all His resources and attributes: His goodness, His wisdom, His peace, His protection, His vision for our lives, and so forth.

Everything we can conceive about God is found in the deep places in Him. You've probably been taught that the Holy Spirit is a comforter, revealer, and enabler, but did you know that He is better than Google—or any other Internet search engine, for that matter?

Let's consider for a moment the apostle Paul's teaching on this subject. In 1 Corinthians 2:7–10, he explains that the Spirit of God goes into the deep places of God and searches out mysteries that the human mind couldn't conceive in a million years. As believers, we receive the Holy Spirit as a matter of God's covenant with those who have come to faith in Jesus Christ. This is an amazing gift, because in the Old Testament, very few got to experience the presence of God: the high priest, once a year on the Day of Atonement; and select individuals, such as Gideon, who, from time to time, received a temporary anointing for a specific task or function. How different it is in the New Testament era. Now, the Holy Spirit lives in the heart of everyone who confesses Jesus as Lord. Those of us who believe on Him have become "temples of the Holy Spirit," His individual dwellings, as the apostle Paul put it. (See 1 Corinthians 3:16; 6:19.)

We are "mobile homes" of the Holy Spirit! The best "search engine" ever actually dwells within our hearts, where He simultaneously explores the depths of God for our benefit. As we are crying out, deep to deep, in moments of great anguish or from beneath a heavy burden, the Spirit of God is conducting a search on our behalf, accessing amazing information that not only soothes our pain and heals us, but also provides divine strategies and insights that take us beyond merely surviving into thriving. My testimony, therefore, is this: When I cried out, God heard me and took me from anguish to abundance.

THE PURPOSE IN OUR PAIN

> God whispers to us in our pleasures, speaks in our conscience, but shouts in our pain: it is His megaphone to rouse a deaf world.[11]
>
> —*C. S. Lewis*

Toward the end of 2008, I was going through some of the worst pain I'd ever experienced. However, I had been in the deep places with God, and so, in the most difficult of times, instead of wallowing in depression, I found myself walking in an abundance of revelation. Instead of feeling confused and bewildered, I gained a focus about what I was to do, where I was to go, and who I was to be. At one point, the direction of God was so clear that I was receiving a new sign every day from the Lord about what to do. The Lord not only healed my hurt but also clothed me with revelation that still carries me today.

In John 16:33, Jesus explained to His disciples that tribulations are bound to come; but, for those who are in Christ, victory is assured because He has overcome the world and all its tribulations.

Before I came to understand this truth, I was really down about my situation, and I gave my dad a call, intending to have a sob session over the phone. What I got was a cold bucket of water tossed in my face. As I was going on and on about how unfairly I was being treated and how I wanted to just leave town, my dad suddenly interrupted me and said, "Son, what do you think makes you so special?"

"Huh?" I said. I wondered if I had heard him correctly, because that was certainly not the answer I had been looking for. I was looking for compassion and a pity party. I guessed my dad had

11. C. S. Lewis, *The Problem of Pain* (New York: HarperOne, 1940, 1996), 91.

forgotten about the Scripture verse that commands us to mourn with those who mourn.

"What makes you so special?" he asked me again. Then he added, "Anyone in the kingdom of God who has ever done anything significant has faced betrayal and abandonment."

I began thinking of all my biblical heroes, and my heart immediately agreed with my dad. I knew he was absolutely right. What made me so special that I would expect to be exempt from having to learn to deal with my problems in a healthy way? There is an anointing that develops when we let God walk us through the difficult seasons of life. The process of encouraging ourselves in the Lord will build our spiritual muscles. When we fixate on God's promises instead of our own problems, God releases a grace upon us to carry larger payloads. And these larger payloads form the tasks that God would have us complete.

> **THERE IS AN ANOINTING THAT DEVELOPS WHEN WE LET GOD WALK US THROUGH THE DIFFICULT SEASONS OF LIFE. THE PROCESS OF ENCOURAGING OURSELVES IN THE LORD WILL BUILD OUR SPIRITUAL MUSCLES. WHEN WE FIXATE ON GOD'S PROMISES INSTEAD OF OUR OWN PROBLEMS, GOD RELEASES A GRACE UPON US TO CARRY LARGER PAYLOADS.**

The anointing always has a purpose assigned to it, and that purpose is never to look holy and powerful in a traditional church setting. In Luke 4:18, Jesus said, *"The Spirit of the Lord is upon Me, because He anointed me to...."* He then went on to list the various purposes that were assigned to His anointing. (See Luke 4:18–19.) When He hears the cry of His people for more anointing, He responds to those prayers by allowing them to develop stronger shoulders for the purpose of carrying greater assignments. It's foolish to think that God gives us problems to teach us, especially when we know He's good all the time; but it's equally foolish to think He won't redeem the tribulations that come to us as a result of our living in a fallen world. God is the ultimate steward. He wouldn't waste five loaves of bread and two fish (see, for example, Mark 6:33–44), and He won't waste the difficulties that come your way, either.

THE SCHOOL OF THE DESERT

> The reason some of us are such poor specimens of Christianity is because we have no Almighty Christ. We have Christian attributes and experiences, but there is no abandonment to Jesus Christ.[12]
>
> —*Oswald Chambers*

Psalm 68:9 tells us that God *"confirmed* [His] *inheritance when it was parched* [*"weary,"* NIV]." The *"inheritance"* to which the writer was referring in this verse is you and I.

Picture this: Here we are on earth, all of us belonging to God, and He decides to confirm the fact that we are His, even when we are parched or weary. Years of serving as a pastor have taught me that some people find it difficult to surrender or submit to the guidance of God when they are in a good place. For some reason, it seems most people can learn only when they are parched or weary due to the challenges of life.

It is when we are going through life's most difficult trials that God tends to get our full attention. Toward the end of 2008, I was a hopeful yet broken man. I know I used up many gallons of gas, aimlessly driving my car around so I could simply have a

12. Oswald Chambers, *My Utmost for His Highest* (Uhrichsville, OH: Barbour Publishing, 1935, 1963), 40.

quiet place to think and try to figure things out. Those were some dark days full of questions. At the same time, I was a getting fresh revelation from heaven, including witty ideas and strategies. It was during my worn-out, weary time that God actually confirmed to me that I was His inheritance—I belonged to Him. He reminded me of who was—His son, His inheritance—and that He was in charge of my life.

Our status in God is not dependent upon whether we are having a good or bad day or month. Regardless of our circumstances, we are a part of God's family, and we have a place in God, with corresponding rights and privileges.

John 1:12 teaches that everyone who believes in Jesus is given the right to become a child of God. Success had made me start to believe I had to work and strive in order to maintain the favor of God. But I soon found myself in a situation where all my hard work didn't count for anything. In fact, my hard work was only making me parched and weary. The only thing I had was my relationship with the Father. I was worn out, but God was confirming to me my sonship.

During this period of weariness, I talked often with my dad. He was a great source of encouragement. A year later, I went home to visit my parents for the holidays, and I was back to my confident self. My dad exclaimed, "Boy, this isn't the person I was talking to last year!" He had no idea how right he was. I was out of the woods. I wasn't fearful anymore. The alarm of the previous year had ended. But something even more profound had fundamentally changed in my heart forever. I had learned that, no matter how successful I became, I should never allow myself to think I needed to strive in order to maintain success in God.

CARNALITY IN PERSPECTIVE

The term "carnality" usually evokes images of sexual misconduct, alcohol abuse, fighting, and other behaviors Christians would identify as obvious sin. The word plainly means "fleshly living." English dictionaries unfortunately give a limited definition of carnality, relating it specifically to sexual appetite, but the Bible gives a broader meaning. The apostle Paul labeled as "carnal" the people who were engaging in arguments over whether it was better to be with him or with Apollos, a fellow worker of Paul's. In other places, the people who were still trying to follow Old Testament law, even after they had received Christ, were called "carnal."

The point is this: *Carnality rears its head whenever people rely on human strength or reasoning rather than God.* When the Lord moved me away from striving, He was actually delivering me from carnality. Striving comes from viewing life through carnal eyes. I was doing work that sounded spiritual, but it was driven by carnal desires. Instead of learning to become more intimate with the Father so I could absorb His heart and thereby access His strength, I had been relying on my own good ideas. At its core, that behavior constituted carnality. Carnal thinking says, "I don't need You, God. I've got this under control. I can handle it myself." Few Christians would make those types of declarations to God, yet so many of our deeds say it loud and clear.

I believe we should war against doing more work just because it seems to be what we're supposed to do. Instead, we should develop the habit of looking to see if the project in front of us is what the Father is up to before we jump into it. For Christians, often, the greatest temptations are not sinful in nature, yet they are carnal. These come in the form of the pressures and expectations that family members, community people, and church members put on them to perform to their standards and engage in every project that sounds like something a Christian ought to be doing. The pressure is particularly acute from the expectations put on us by the world. Feeling the need to defend Jesus to the world, we risk overextending ourselves as we endeavor to prove that Jesus is good and that His people can be trusted. We end up bowing our knees to the world's expectations and allowing society to become a puppeteer controlling our mission.

> **FOR CHRISTIANS, OFTEN, THE GREATEST TEMPTATIONS ARE NOT SINFUL IN NATURE, YET THEY ARE CARNAL. THESE COME IN THE FORM OF THE PRESSURES AND EXPECTATIONS THAT FAMILY MEMBERS, COMMUNITY PEOPLE, AND CHURCH MEMBERS PUT ON THEM TO PERFORM TO THEIR STANDARDS.**

When this type of capitulation occurs, the world subtly starts dictating what the church will and won't do. One thing I love about Jesus is that He took His marching orders from the Father alone. His cousin John the Baptist was locked in prison and scheduled to die, yet Jesus didn't go visit him, much less break him out. The snub offended John, but Jesus stayed put because He did only what His Father told Him to do.

On another occasion, Jesus purposely stayed away from his dying friend Lazarus for three days, to the dismay of the man's sisters, Martha and Mary. When Jesus finally showed up, Mary was furious with Him. He didn't explain His tardiness but simply commanded that the stone be rolled away from the opening of Lazarus's tomb. (See John 11:1–40.) Jesus then prayed aloud, saying, "*Father, I thank You that You have heard Me. I knew that You always hear Me; but because of the people standing around I said it, so that they may believe that You sent Me*" (John 11:41–42). Then He raised Lazarus from the dead, partnering with what the Father was doing.

He had prayed out loud so the people within earshot would understand that He was not going to do what they wanted but only what His Father wanted. Jesus was radical in His obedience and totally free from outside pressure to perform for anyone.

There are so many demands placed on us, but we can't afford to bow to them, because a vicious performance spirit gets released in our lives when we find ourselves attempting to meet the expectations and needs of anyone but our Father God. Performance has an insatiable appetite, seeking to devour all our time and energy. We complete one project and feel great about it, but then another project comes, and, soon after that, another one. Suddenly, we've become someone who "gets things done." Awards and accolades accompany such a reputation, but we can never say no, because we have an image to uphold. We end up parched and exhausted, trying to maintain a reputation in our community instead of trying to expand God's kingdom.

PERFORMANCE HAS AN INSATIABLE APPETITE, SEEKING TO DEVOUR ALL OUR TIME AND ENERGY.

Many churches and leaders sacrifice their original fire and vision over time by taking up projects that, in spite of their legitimacy and worth, aren't what the Father is doing. People create jobs the Father never intended for them to have, and they end up doing exhausting work instead of blessing what the Father is doing, partnering with Him, and getting refreshed all the time they are doing it.

Partnering with the Father leaves us refreshed. In partnership with God, there is no getting parched or weary. We may require occasional breaks for rest and rejuvenation, but we don't experience internal burnout.

When I hear about church leaders suffering from burnout, I wonder if they were carrying burdens God never told them to pick up in the first place. Bill Johnson once told me that the way he checks to see whether a person is called of God to do something is by looking to see if that person is refreshed or worn out after doing the job. He said, "If people are worn out from doing it, the chances are that they were never supposed to be doing it in the first place." When we partner with God, we are free from performing and striving. We actually get refreshed in the process of pursuing what God is up to.

I was parched and weary, but the Father came and confirmed me as His inheritance in the worst of my days, in the time when I didn't feel as if I belonged to anyone. He showed me that my life was secured, not because of my hard work but because He loves me as His son.

There are moments, in our worst frustrations, that God exploits to show off His grace and tender mercy. He confirms and affirms us as His inheritance, and lets us know we're going to be just fine. God is raising up people who have learned, from suffering, to look beyond the hills, not just for help but for confirmation that God's hand is on them to do great exploits.

THE NEW REVIVALISTS

I believe we are in the midst of a generation of believers who have learned to deal with their disappointments and failures in a godly way. These revivalists are doing a good job managing the tension of simultaneously living with the most loving Father and confronting life's challenges. Previous generations were made up of so many who would harbor criticisms and setbacks, using them as fuel to spur inferior responses, such as working harder, being more diligent, exerting more energy, and performing better. In many cases, these individuals became more vulnerable to further frustration because, unbeknownst to them, a spirit of performance had crept into their lives. Today, however, more people are allowing their disappointments to draw them nearer to the Father's heart, fueling their passion to abandon the ankle-deep-only experiences in God's river so that they might jump in over their heads, reaching the place where they can no longer control themselves but must be carried wherever the river takes them. They've seen the life that flows in those depths, and they have followed the Lord into places they had previously only imagined. These are the revivalists who aren't concerned with appearance, protocol, and personal fame. Instead, they exist to make Jesus famous, and they've given themselves with abandon to the fresh fire from God. These men and women are willing to pay the cost, even if it results in betrayal, misunderstanding, and persecution.

This hungry group wants to see the fulfillment of Habakkuk 2:14—they want to see the knowledge of the glory of God filling the earth.

They are African-American, White, Latino, Asian; they are people from every race.

These emerging revivalists are not reducing the mission to church pastors, preachers, and apostles. Rather, they sense God's commissioning on their own lives to be agents of change in the marketplace, in schools—everywhere they go.

AN UNSTOPPABLE RIVER

The Grand Canyon is regarded as one of the Seven Natural Wonders of the World. Geologists tell us the canyon was formed by the Colorado River's running through those rocks for millions of years. The continual flow of water broke through some of the hardest places, creating one of the most breathtaking places on the planet.

We believers have an eternal river that flows out of our bellies, and even the hardest of places can't resist this river. The river of God is breaking forth into places long assumed impenetrable and creating something beautiful.

I believe that the strongholds of this world—from Hollywood culture to Wall Street corruption to New-Age mysticism—all are bowing the knee to the name of Jesus, and that the river of God is being released in greater measure.

As believers, we have been commissioned to carry the anointing that we've received through great tribulation into dry places longing for a drink.

All over the world, this is happening so that we can declare with David, "I believe I will see the goodness of the Lord in the land of the living." (See Psalm 27:13.)

Young or old, we are privileged to be alive at this time in history, to see things that the prophets of former times only dreamed about.

Whatever the cost, it is well worth paying for whatever we receive from God in the exchange.

4

USE IT OR LOSE IT

During my time as an undergraduate at Howard University in Washington, D.C., I worked at the Pentagon for the Department of Defense. Part of the pay system involved something called "accrual hours." All of us accrued vacation time, sick days, and personal days based on the number of consecutive hours of work we logged. Working forty consecutive hours—five days in a row—earned about three hours' time off. At the end of the fiscal year, whatever accrued hours we hadn't used would be forfeited. "Use it or lose it!" we would say.

In Luke chapter 19, Jesus told a story in order to illustrate God's heart regarding stewardship and increase. The disciples thought that the kingdom of God was going to appear immediately. They were still missing the point concerning God's coming kingdom. Like many others of their time, they were looking for a physical kingdom to appear, and a Messiah to overthrow Rome—with a full menu of soldiers, revolution, political upheaval, coups d'état...the works. However, God's kingdom is not like earthly kingdoms; its systems and rules are completely different from the systems of our world.

Instead of answering their concerns directly, Jesus did what He always did as a master teacher: He told a story. In the parable, a nobleman went away to receive a kingdom for himself, and then he returned. Before he'd left town, he'd given each of his slaves ten minas—a unit of money—and had told them to do business with that money until he returned from his journey. Upon his return, he found that the first slave had doubled his money by adding ten additional minas; the second had earned a 50-percent profit of five minas. The third slave, however, brought in no return on the nobleman's investment, because he had chosen not to do anything with the money that had been entrusted to him.

One key to understanding this parable is to comprehend the simple fact that the master utilized his servants to get business done. There are many in the church today who don't believe that God wants to work with His people. They have bought into the notion that God's sovereignty rules out the need for any human intervention. But I don't see that as God's heart. Throughout Scripture, we see many instances of God allowing men and women to be involved in shaping the course of human history. The psalmist wrote that God has entrusted the earth to men. (See Psalm 115:16.) Yet many Christians believe their contribution doesn't matter. Far too many people gravitate toward the lie that God doesn't really need us to get the job done. Technically, that is true, but we shouldn't stop there. We all know the Creator of the universe could do everything on His own, but He invites us to embrace a higher truth: He chooses to partner with us in order to expand His kingdom on earth.

> **WE ALL KNOW THE CREATOR OF THE UNIVERSE COULD DO EVERYTHING ON HIS OWN, BUT HE INVITES US TO EMBRACE A HIGHER TRUTH: HE CHOOSES TO PARTNER WITH US IN ORDER TO EXPAND HIS KINGDOM ON EARTH.**

FIXING THE LIGHT BULBS

When my son, Troy, was around five or six years old, he loved making trips with me to the local Home Depot to purchase things I needed for various household projects. He had fun shopping with me, but his greater joy was getting home and helping me with the projects. If there was a new light bulb I had to install, I'd tighten it until it needed only four or five more rotations, and I'd save those for Troy. I'd call him over and say, "Troy, I need you, man. It's your shift."

What a joy it was for me to see his face—and the bulb—light up when he finished the job. I would get such a kick out of hearing Troy run downstairs to brag to everyone within earshot that he had just finished fixing the lamp. Technically, I didn't need his help finishing the job, but he needed me to need him to finish the job. His sense of significance and self-worth was being formed in the moments when his dad asked for his help. Meanwhile, I experienced the parental pleasure of witnessing my child's development firsthand.

The way God has decided to live with us is very similar. In His sovereignty, He has chosen to call us in for the last few "turns of the light bulb" so that we can grow in our own sense of self-worth and also share with Him in the joy of a job well done. When we buy into the religious lie that God doesn't want us involved in His work, we deprive ourselves of the chance to work alongside Him and share in the joy of a finished job, which has been His plan from the beginning of time. I believe we also short-change God from taking pleasure in His children.

WHAT'S IN YOUR HANDS?

In the parable of the minas in Luke 19, we see partnership; we also see productivity. The master gave each of his slaves ten minas. One key to experiencing the culture of heaven is to recognize that every person on planet Earth has been given a gift from the Father. In Luke 19, the nobleman did not invest equally in his slaves, which illustrates the truth that our gifts, and their sizes, vary. Regardless of the size of the investment you've received from God, the point is that God is looking to see if you will do something with what you've been given.

When God spoke to Moses and instructed him to lead Israel out of bondage in Egypt, Moses responded with a sequence of excuses—reasons why he couldn't possibly be the one God wanted to use. He listed shortcoming after shortcoming. The Lord's response was simple: "Moses, what's in your hands?" He asked. (See Exodus 4.)

The challenge for God's people is to take inventory of what they have in their hands already. God is able to accomplish so much with even the little we think we possess. He is well aware of our shortcomings and challenges—even more so than we are—and yet He still chooses us.

In Deuteronomy 7, God speaks to Israel, saying that they weren't chosen because they were the largest or the strongest nation but because He simply wanted to display His love for them. It becomes arrogant to try to explain to the One who created us the reasons why He can't use us. Again, God is fully aware of our weaknesses, but He loves to take our little and turn it into much. He knows we have only one mina, and He's looking to see if we'll be faithful with that small investment so that He can entrust us with the right to rule over even more. Let's not focus on the size of our measure; let's focus on His power to bring increase.

QUALIFIED TO HANDLE INCREASE

> If God is your partner, make your plans BIG!
> —*D. L. Moody*

The emergence of "faith teachers" has blessed the body of Christ immeasurably by unearthing the revelation of abundance promised to all believers. When I first became a Christian, I listened frequently to the teaching of Kenneth Hagin Sr. "Dad" Hagin could arguably be regarded as the father of the modern faith movement.

One of the great statements Brother Hagin would make was, "You can fall into the ditch on either side of the road!" He meant that even true, biblical teaching, if unbalanced, can lead people astray.

The church has encountered something of a dilemma over the last twenty years. Many people in the body of Christ heard the prosperity message from the faith teachers, but they didn't pay attention to the full message that was being communicated. They heard only the part that says, "God wants to bless you." What they didn't hear was the other side of that revelation: God is looking to see how we will manage what we have in our hands right now, and, based on that, He will determine whether ours is the kind of character that can not only receive a blessing but also sustain it for the generations to follow.

GOD IS LOOKING TO SEE HOW WE WILL MANAGE WHAT WE HAVE IN OUR HANDS RIGHT NOW, AND, BASED ON THAT, HE WILL DETERMINE WHETHER OURS IS THE KIND OF CHARACTER THAT CAN NOT ONLY RECEIVE A BLESSING BUT ALSO SUSTAIN IT FOR THE GENERATIONS TO FOLLOW.

When the church develops a consumer mentality, it actually negates what it has been called to accomplish. The goal of consumerism is to accumulate more and more stuff; in God's economy, the more you give away, the more qualified you become to receive more. (See John 12:25.) Faithful stewardship, in the kingdom of God, is simply being willing to release whatever is in our hands, whether big or small.

In the parable in Luke 19, the slave who produced ten additional minas was given the remaining minas from the slave who hadn't done anything. One slave showed himself qualified to handle increase; the other showed himself incapable of being faithful with even the little he'd started out with.

The reality is that it is the Father's pleasure to give us the kingdom. (See Luke 12:32.) He didn't spare His own Son, so how will He not graciously give us all things? (See Romans 8:32.)

The exchange rate for our faithfulness is unparalleled. The slaves were given authority over ten cities based on their management of ten minas. Where are we ever going to find a better deal?

KEEP YOUR FAUCET ON!

The Father delights in blessing us, but He is more interested in who we are than what blessings we're chasing after.

Jesus's disciples were looking for the kingdom, and they wanted it right then and there. Even today, a culture of instant gratification pervades the church. But the Lord is raising a generation of people who will hear His heart and will focus on being faithful in releasing what they have. God is still asking His people the same question He asked Moses when he didn't think he had enough in him to lead the Israelites out of captivity in Egypt: "What is in your hands?"

When I understood this, I immediately started praying for other people as if I already had the power I longed for. It really clicked one day while I was shopping with a friend at Wal-Mart. I had been asking the Father for an anointing that would cure cerebral palsy. That day in Wal-Mart, I saw a little girl in a wheelchair stricken with this horrible disease. There was no great stirring in my soul; I just understood that I needed to use what I had. I approached the little girl's mother and asked for permission to pray for her daughter. She obliged, and I began to lay hands on her daughter and to pray.

After several minutes, absolutely nothing had happened, but I wasn't deflated at all. I grabbed my bags, told the family about our church, and blessed them as I left the store. As soon as I stepped out the door, I heard the Lord say to me, "Oh, I see you've turned your faucet on." I instantly knew what He meant. He was saying that my choice to pray for the girl was like turning on a faucet, and that if I would just remain faithful in keeping my "faucet" on, then the waters would start to flow. How soon and how much really isn't up to us—that's God's business. Our job is to just make sure the faucet stays on.

Ever since I came to this understanding, I have prayed, acted, and lived with greater boldness; I have also seen more miracles this past year alone than in my entire life. After that episode at Wal-Mart, I got to witness a woman being healed of cerebral palsy, and, in the process, the Lord reminded me of what I was after.

While working on this book, I had an experience that definitely qualifies as miraculous. I traveled by plane to Seoul, South Korea, in a first-class seat—not because I paid extra but because God wanted me to see His kingdom in operation.

At the airport, when I arrived at the gate, I approached the counter and asked an airline representative if it would be possible to upgrade my seat from coach to business or first class by using miles I had earned. The airline representative immediately informed me that even if my miles were compatible with the airline—they weren't—my request would be impossible to fulfill. All the seats were sold, and the flight was full.

It seemed there was no hope for an upgrade, so I mentally prepared myself for a fifteen-hour plane ride in coach. As I was waiting for boarding to begin, I went to the restroom. Another man followed me in, and it was obvious he was trying to make eye contact with me. I tried to ignore him, but this man was so blatant in his advances, I couldn't help but notice.

Keeping my gaze averted, I quickly left the restroom. About thirty minutes and one Starbucks venti latte later, I was back in the restroom when, out of the corner of my eye, I saw the same guy approaching me, drawing even closer this time. His presence made me very uncomfortable, so I quickly finished up and got out of there as fast as I could. I saw him come out of the restroom and disappear into a crowd of people waiting at a nearby gate. I felt relieved. *Good,* I thought to myself. *I'm so glad he's not on this flight. That's all I need—fifteen hours on a flight with a guy who keeps coming at me in bathrooms.*

As I sat there grumbling to myself, I couldn't believe it—the Lord started to impress upon me certain details about the man. *God, You have got to be joking!* I said silently. *You actually want me to go prophesy to him? Come on, Lord—don't make me go minister to this guy!*

That's when God allowed me to see the man as He saw him—a broken, lost, and confused son.

The Father gave me His loving eyes, and instantly I felt a sense of compassion for him.

Faith works by love. I had one last bargaining chip with God, so I said, "Okay. If You really want me to bless this guy, You'll have to allow me to see him again in the crowd. Besides, Lord, I've got to see if I can get my aisle seat changed to a window seat." I wanted to be able to at least lean against the window and get some sleep during the flight. I heard Him say, "If you take care of My business, I'll take care of yours."

Just as He finished saying this, the guy popped out of nowhere into my line of vision. He disappeared again, only to pop right back into view a second time. I mustered my courage, walked over, and introduced myself. His name was Andre, and he was traveling home to Germany. He spoke excellent English, and so, after a moment of awkwardness, I told him that God loved him very much. I began to share things with him about his own childhood, such as his parents' rejection of him. I told him that he had a love for children—a love that was a gift from God, and a gift God wanted to use. He shared that he had worked with children for sixteen years, and that's what he really loved and wanted to get back to doing. I told him that he had heard about Jesus Christ but had never paid attention, and now God wanted his full attention in order to have a relationship with him. He revealed that he actually lived on the campus of an evangelical Christian college in Germany.

By now, I had his attention, and he was nearly in tears. I prayed for him and blessed him, then went to board my flight. When I got to the door, I asked one of the flight attendants about the possibility of getting a window seat. The woman apologized, saying there was nothing she could do, because all the seats were taken. Just then, her colleague standing nearby said something to her in Korean, and then she handed me a new ticket for seat 17A. "I think you're going to like that seat," she told me.

I couldn't help feeling incredulous as I boarded the plane. I couldn't locate seat 17A, so I motioned for one of the flight attendants to help me. She looked at my ticket and then said, "Please, sir, follow me upstairs. You are seated in first class."

If it weren't for the suspicion I would have aroused, I would have shouted a victory cry for all to hear. Instead, I just called a friend and gave them the testimony to share with the church in my absence. I am sure they all shouted for me!

Jesus said that living waters would flow out of the bellies of those who believe in Him. (See John 7:38 KJV.) All He needs is people who will radically obey Him, and turn their faucets on.

Turn your faucet on, and keep it on!

TAKING IT TO THE HOOD

I have learned to celebrate the "minor" miracles in preparation for "major" ones. I faithfully use what little I have so that I can be worthy of more. I celebrate wildly, even if someone tells me that God healed his headache, because I don't want my heart to become indifferent to instances of His moving in our midst, whether those instances be great or small. I believe the way we celebrate and honor the seemingly minor victories sets us up for celebrations and breakthroughs in major areas.

I've got a dream in my heart for an anointing to destroy sickle cell anemia, cancer, and asthma. I desire that anyone who comes to me with any of those diseases be healed 100 percent of the time when I pray for him or her. I believe that by being faithful over the smaller anointing and faithfully praying for colds, headaches, sore backs, and aching muscles, I am being prepared to walk into the reality of that dream. In fact, I have a personal goal of taking a risk for God every day so I can always be using what little I have. I want the world to encounter God when they encounter me, and that starts by my giving away what I have, no matter how little I think it is.

Years ago, my son and I were in Dorchester, Massachusetts, picking up a spiritual daughter named Cristina to drive her back to college. She lives with her mother and two brothers in a part of Dorchester that has its urban challenges; in other words, it's the "hood." As we were loading Cristina's stuff, I noticed three young men across the street hanging out and smoking marijuana. You don't normally approach people when they are in this condition, but my heavenly obligation was larger than my human fears, so I decided to take a risk. I just felt compelled to go and speak to them.

These guys must have thought I was some nut job, because, in the hood, you do not approach random people. If you have ever lived in a tough neighborhood, you know this is a dangerous and borderline-crazy thing to do. But I went to them and said these words: "Brothers, excuse me. I know this is going to sound weird, but I just want to tell you that I see something in your lives. You guys are leaders with a godly destiny, and God has great plans for you."

I began to prophesy to them and to release blessings over them. Amazingly, the Lord gave me prophetic words for each of them. These three young men, clearly high on marijuana, had the Spirit of God invade their party and pull them out of their stupor. Their high quickly departed, and I watched as they buckled and bowed to the presence of God, right there on Clarkson Street in the "hood," on a Friday afternoon.

I think that was a good place for a revival.

A RETURN ON THE INVESTMENT

> One of the principal rules of religion is, to lose no occasion of serving God. And, since He is invisible to our eyes, we are to serve Him in our neighbor; which He receives as if done to Himself in person, standing visibly before us.[13]
>
> —*John Wesley*

I know God has anointed all of us to bring that kind of kingdom reality crashing into the inferior reality of earth. We all have a mandate to cause heaven to invade earth. This is the type of lifestyle we are wired for. This kind of thing is not meant to be an occasional event but an everyday mind-set. We are a people who have received salvation, which is the greatest sign and wonder ever experienced, and God is looking for a harvest of fruit from that salvation seed. Salvation is not the end but the beginning. Jesus asked, "When I return, will I find such faith?" (See Luke 18:8.)

13. John Wesley, *A Plain Account of Christian Perfection* (New Kensington, PA: Whitaker House, 2015), 131.

He is looking to see what we do with the life He has released to us. This is the obligation. This is the payment. The return on God's investment is the lives we touch with the presence of the Lord.

> **WE ARE A PEOPLE WHO HAVE RECEIVED SALVATION, WHICH IS THE GREATEST SIGN AND WONDER EVER EXPERIENCED, AND GOD IS LOOKING FOR A HARVEST OF FRUIT FROM THAT SALVATION SEED. SALVATION IS NOT THE END BUT THE BEGINNING.**

Deuteronomy 7:22 is a fascinating statement made by Moses as he addressed the second generation of Israelites who had come out of Egypt and would actually enter Canaan, the land of promise. He issued them a warning, of sorts, saying, in effect, "I have got a promise from God for you. It is a promise of this new land, but God is not going to give it to you all at once. He is going to give it to you little by little, because wild animals will overtake the land, and will be too much for you." In other words, "It is the heart of the Father to bless you, but it is more the heart of the Father to make you into a people who can sustain the blessing."

What the Lord is working in us is not just the ability to pray for people and see the wheelchairs emptied. He is also working within us character and godliness so we won't get excited about the empty wheelchairs and forget the One who emptied them in the first place.

Too often, we hear stories of people succeeding at a rate that outpaced their ability to manage success well. They do not have the internal structure to support the success in a way that allows them to pass down that reality to the next generation.

As we learn to work with the Holy Spirit and freely give what we have, the valuable character traits that the Father wants to form in us will become part of our core character along the way.

TWELVE BASKETS LEFT OVER

Never forget this: Absolutely nothing is ever wasted in the kingdom of God.

Up to now, we've talked about stewarding gifts and talents. We need to realize that we are also called to steward the difficulties that life thrusts our way. When I was an unbeliever, it seemed as if the problems I faced came without rhyme or reason. When I became a Christian, however, I realized that even my difficulties started working for me. My problems had a purpose. As I wrote in the last chapter, I don't believe that God strikes His people with difficulties, but I do know with certainty that He allows the challenges we face. Regardless of where you are, theologically speaking—whether you believe God causes problems or allows them—the point is, no one is exempt from facing extreme difficulties. Our job is to learn how to manage them well.

We learn, from parables like the one Jesus told in Luke 19, that God is the ultimate manager of His resources, and that He wastes nothing. When the young man came to Jesus with five loaves of bread and two fish, He used what He had. (See Mark 6:33–44; John 6:1–14.) It didn't seem like much, but Jesus blessed the food, and I believe He was really responding to the act of stewardship on the young man's part. The boy's instinctive faith in the power of Christ caused him to take a risk by giving away what little he had as an act of stewardship. This simple act unlocked an atmospheric transformation that invited a grace for increase to invade a context of need.

When we are willing to take simple risks, the culture of heaven invades earth in extraordinary ways. In that charged climate, all the disciples started handing out the food, and they watched it multiply, going from not enough to more than enough.

Not only did the food increase, but the miracles did, as well. Every disciple got to participate in the working of a miracle.

I believe God wants to release an anointing that is too powerful for any one man to carry. Whole congregations are going to come into this anointing and change the economic condition of cities, educational systems—every area of influence.

Even after the miraculous feeding of the 5,000, there were twelve baskets left over, and the Lord made sure to collect them. He is the ultimate steward of resources, and He does not waste a thing.

> **GOD IS THE ULTIMATE STEWARD OF RESOURCES, AND HE DOES NOT WASTE A THING.**

All this happened in the first place because one young man chose not to allow a problem to define his circumstances.

TURNING IT ALL AROUND

> [Trials] are meant to be our teachers, but at the end of the day, it is up to us to choose what kind of students we want to be.[14]
>
> —*Lisa Bevere*

One of the greatest tragedies in the church is that people judge themselves by the apparent lack in their lives, instead of judging themselves by the measure that God's already given them.

In Romans 12:3, the apostle Paul says that we should not think of ourselves more highly than we ought, but rather in accordance with the measure of faith we have been given. It's destructive to think of ourselves based on what we do not have or what we merely

14. Lisa Bevere, *Without Rival* (Grand Rapids, MI: Revell, 2016), 175.

pretend to have. When people lower the standard of what God has said about them, and develop a habit of downplaying their worth just so they can sound holy and noble, they are practicing false humility. The real place of strength is defining ourselves according to God's perspective. When we get a true picture of our lives, we realize that even the direst circumstances we have experienced were redemptive in God's economy.

Scripture teaches that we are the salt of the earth and the light of the world; we are a city on a hill that cannot be hidden. (See Matthew 5:13–14.) When we experience challenges and difficult changes, God actually wants to redeem those times and to give us strength to use them so that we might become a fragrant offering in the lives of other people going through similar situations. The persecutions we've suffered have eternal value. Our own suffering creates in us a compassion for others in similar situations, and it enables us to bless them in a far more profound way than anyone else can.

WHEN WE EXPERIENCE CHALLENGES AND DIFFICULT CHANGES, GOD ACTUALLY WANTS TO REDEEM THOSE TIMES AND TO GIVE US STRENGTH TO USE THEM SO THAT WE MIGHT BECOME A FRAGRANT OFFERING IN THE LIVES OF OTHER PEOPLE GOING THROUGH SIMILAR SITUATIONS.

Years ago, I met Kai Leigh Harriott, a beautiful little girl who grew to become a beautiful young woman. She and her family were members of a church I helped plant in Boston. Kai had these big dimples that showed up all day because she was always smiling. She wore her hair in pigtails and was always immaculately dressed. Whenever she entered a room, the whole place would light up.

When Kai was four years old, she was struck by a stray bullet in Roxbury, Massachusetts, and became paralyzed from the sternum down. Soon after this tragic event, she and her mother, Tonya David, went to the prison to visit the gunman, and they forgave him. All the news media outlets in the Boston area covered this extraordinary turn of events. Kai and Tonya also started a foundation called Forgiveness Is the Way, and they now travel all over the nation, speaking the message of forgiveness.

Every time they'd come into the church sanctuary, I'd get rocked by God because of the privilege of being in the company of people who have decided to take their bitter circumstances, redefine them, and use them to bless others.

I would often ask Kai to lay her hands on me and pray, because I think everyone could use more grace to rename our world, and Kai certainly carries a huge measure of it.

When Adam walked in fellowship with God in the garden of Eden, he carried the ability to name things whatever he saw fit to name them. Through the last Adam, Jesus Christ, our fellowship with God has been restored, and we have been given the same authority to name things according to our heart.

In life, persecution and challenges are like a double-edged sword. One side of the blade creates the immediate, painful impact we experience. But the other side is more dangerous, because it attempts to define who we are.

I know people who have been defined by failure and disappointment. Difficulties hurt when they happen to us, but we get to choose whether we'll be cut even deeper by the other side of the blade.

God has given us the power to turn that blade back onto the challenge itself, so that, instead of the challenge defining us, we define it, and witness the glory that can come from the most difficult of experiences. In effect, we have an anointing to use our persecutions as places of stewardship.

In my ministry travels, I have gotten to meet many people from varying backgrounds and experiences. Some are new to the faith, just learning the things of God; others have been walking with the Lord for many years. Of the latter group, I am most impressed by those who have experienced setbacks in their journey, yet remain passionate and hopeful. It's as if life threw extreme difficulties at them, and, somehow, instead of being mortally wounded, they learned to use the challenges to gain more strength.

I believe God is sending a wave of fresh strength to the whole body of Christ, causing people to take their old hurts and use them as launchpads into new levels of glory and power.

Remember "Use it or lose it"? We must choose to use, or lose, everything we have—from God-given gifts, talents, and abilities, to the extreme disappointments and setbacks that life throws our way.

My encouragement to you: If you want to live in the culture of heaven, then choose to "use it."

5

HANGING OUT WITH THE ANOINTING

I once heard a preacher tell a story of a farmer who entered his mule in the Kentucky Derby. When asked why he would do such a thing, he answered, "I thought the exposure would do him a world of good!"

If we're going to increase in the anointing and see more of the culture of heaven, it's vital that we spend time around people who are doing what we dream about doing, and that we open our lives to people who carry a greater anointing than we do. Joshua was mentored by Moses and became a great leader himself. Clearly, the exposure to such a spiritual giant as Moses did Joshua a world of good.

Throughout my life, one of the most important and most consistent features has been the series of wonderful mentors God has placed in my path. I've had three fathers who have covered the span of my life. My dad, Pastor Richard Goode, is an incredibly godly man. He was my first pastor, and he taught me to be a man. He loved my mom with all his heart, and he nurtured my sister and me with such care. I learned how to do life by watching my dad every day.

When I recommitted my life to Christ in 1993, I moved to Boston, Massachusetts, for a fresh start. I started attending a vibrant church where the pastor embraced me as if I had been his own son. He then trained me in my formative years in ministry, teaching me much about leading a church and being a man of God. The years I spent with Bishop Gideon Thompson were invaluable to me, and I still draw strength from my time spent with him.

Years later, I took a trip that ended up bringing a third spiritual father into my life. When I had moved into a new phase of ministry and was helping to plant a church in Rhode Island, I went to visit a dear friend in Pasadena, California, for his fortieth birthday party. As we turned onto my friend's street, he pointed to a house and said, matter-of-factly, "Pastor Ché Ahn lives there." Pastor Ché Ahn is the senior leader of HRock Church in Pasadena, and he is a part of the Revival Alliance Network. An incredibly anointed leader, he is also the apostolic leader of the Harvest International Ministry (HIM) Network, which comprises over 25,000 churches globally. He is a unique apostolic leader—one whom I had been reading about and following for months. At one point, I had said to myself, *I hope one day I get to meet Pastor Ché*. When I saw his house, the Lord spoke to my heart and told me to go and knock on his door, and to be bold.

As soon as I climbed out of my friend's car, I nervously walked to Pastor Ché's house. The closer I got, the faster my heart raced, but I kept hearing God say, "Be bold." After several minutes of my knocking, Pastor Ché himself answered the door. I introduced myself, explaining that I was planting a church in Providence, Rhode Island, and that I'd wanted to meet him because I had long admired him from afar. Not only did he greet me, but he ended up prophesying and pronouncing an apostolic blessing over my life and church. As I was leaving, he thanked me for stopping by. "Thank you for your *boldness*," he added.

Soon after that initial meeting, I returned to Pasadena for a HIM conference, where I got to know Pastor Ché even better.

Several months after that, he and his wife, Sue, came to minister at our church in Rhode Island and spent time with our team. We have since joined the HIM Network.

Pastor Ché has had a significant influence on my life and on the life of our ministry. I know that much of the anointing we carry is due to the time we spend routinely with pastors Ché and Sue Ahn.

Early on, our church convened for services in a school. When we were searching for a permanent meeting location, Pastor Ché told me of his own experience pastoring a church in a rented facility. He recounted the challenges of setting up before services and breaking down afterward, and the issues they had with the landlords. In the middle of this time of struggling, God suddenly blessed them with the magnificent facility they now have. After sharing his story, Pastor Ché said he felt led by God to lay hands on me for property.

Within weeks of Pastor Ché's laying hands on me, we were blessed with a 30,000-square-foot facility that has one of the best parking situations of any church I've seen. We were able to do a complete renovation of the building. All this happened within the first two years of our ministry. I'm confident that the anointing Pastor Ché gained from his own property struggle was imparted to our ministry, and we were the better for it.

There truly is a transfer of anointing that comes to people who are hungry for that which others carry.

For me, pastors Ché and Sue Ahn are some of the most loving and gracious people I've ever encountered. They are real spiritual parents and mentors in our world, and I love spending time with them.

PUSHING PAST THE OFFENSE

Relating to carriers of the anointing may not always be as easy as it was for me with the Ahns. There are times when God will cause you to encounter a person who carries something you're extremely hungry for, but the person with that anointing is not as congenial to deal with. In those seasons, your spiritual maturity will enable you to recognize the personal shortcomings but not get so hung up on them that you end up forfeiting an important transfer of the anointing.

The concept of transferring the anointing is a big deal. When I first began moving in the realm of healing, I would see people healed of migraine headaches, sore backs, and aching knees. These occurrences ignited within me a desire to see an increase in healings. I wanted to go after blind eyes and deaf ears. I learned that spending time with people who moved in those miracles was important, because the anointing they carried could be transferred.

I started spending more time with people who saw the types of miracles I desired on a regular basis, and I soon noticed these miracles begin to increase in my own life. First, I saw a man healed of deafness in his left ear. Next, a woman with cancer came to our church. We prayed for her, and two weeks later I received a report that her cancer had stopped spreading.

I know that one of the reasons these healings intensified is because I had set my heart on spending more time with people who were walking in what I wanted. I haven't distanced myself from anyone who isn't going after the same things as I am, yet I'm aware that I have to be a good steward of my time, and be sure to spend the majority of it around people who are more advanced than I am in certain areas, such as the anointing.

When I hear that someone is consistently seeing people get healed of a particular disease, I often search out him or her in an effort to receive impartation, because he or she is walking in an anointing that I want in my own life.

We see a precedent of the transfer of anointing in the Bible, with the prophet Elijah and his protégé, Elisha. In a time of crisis for Israel, King Jehoshaphat heard that Elisha used to pour water on Elijah's hands, and the king concluded that the young man must carry a similar anointing to Elijah because of the time he had spent with him. King Jehoshaphat knew Elijah's anointing had been transferred to Elisha. Sure enough, Elisha had received a mantle from Elijah because he had purposed in his heart to stay close to Elijah no matter what. Elijah told Elisha, "If you see me when I depart, then you will have what you say." (See 2 Kings 2:10.) But for the next several ministry trips, it seemed that Elijah was trying to get rid of Elisha. Elisha had his heart set on Elijah's anointing, so he didn't allow himself to be distracted by Elijah's personal issues. He was mature enough to abide Elijah's quirks so as not to miss that which Elijah was about to transmit to him. Elisha chased Elijah to four cities and ignored all his rejections because he was so hungry for the anointing on Elijah's life.

For Elisha, the double-portion anointing was the goal, and he was not going to let himself get sidetracked by Elijah's hang-ups. The first time Elijah told him to leave and not follow him, most people would have packed their belongings and simply gone back home dejected. But not Elisha. He saw beyond Elijah's obvious lack of social skills, focused on what Elijah carried, and locked his gaze on that.

MANY PEOPLE MISS OUT ON AVAILABLE GRACE FROM GOD BECAUSE THE ANOINTING THEY ARE AFTER IS WRAPPED IN AN "OFFENSIVE" PACKAGE. SADLY, THE KINGDOM OF GOD IS LITTERED WITH PEOPLE WHO ARE ENTIRELY TOO SENSITIVE FOR THEIR OWN GOOD.

Many people miss out on available grace from God because the anointing they are after is wrapped in an "offensive" package. Sadly, the kingdom of God is littered with people who are entirely too sensitive for their own good. We want the kind of anointing we see operating in the lives and ministries of great men and women of God, but we want our leaders squeaky-clean. We don't want them to offend us or disappoint us or let us down. Yet our expectation is not very realistic, because all Christian leaders are still human beings, subject to the same flaws as everyone else.

Don't get me wrong; we certainly don't tolerate or wink at the sins of anointed leaders. We must demand personal integrity and purity from our leaders; and those who fail in these areas will receive judgment from the Lord. But it's redemptive judgment we're talking about here. With a redemptive view of life, we don't seize upon a leader's failures and weaknesses as a reason to demean and dishonor him or her. For reasons known only to Him, God entrusts flawed human beings with His power, and the power-hungry have to choose whether they really want that power.

The Kingdom culture celebrates people for who they are without stumbling over who they are not.[15]
—*Bill Johnson*

When you are going after a particular person's anointing, many times, you have to fight through personality and personal mistakes to get to what you want. But the double-portion anointing you receive is well worth the fight. Fighting through those challenges becomes easier when you carry enough maturity to recognize the inherent anointing that accompanies the office a leader holds. The man may be flawed, but the office is still sanctified.

Consider David, who refused to do anything to disparage Saul, even though he was well aware of Saul's failures as a man. David respected Saul's office as king. That office held a spiritual power that David dared not violate.

---

15. Eric Johnson and Bill Johnson, *Momentum* (Shippensburg, PA: Destiny Image Publishers, Inc., 2011), 73.

In the United States, we have three branches of government: the judicial branch, or the Supreme Court; the legislative branch, which is made up of the Senate and Congress; and the executive branch, which is embodied in the president. No matter who is serving as president, that person embodies a branch of our government. An attack against him or her is really an attack against the entire U.S. government.

I believe that, in a similar way, when we allow ourselves to make careless judgments about Christian leaders, the angelic forces of God go into "high alert" because someone is making verbal assaults against offices of the government of God.

In light of this, it is possible that many of us need to reevaluate how we've treated certain leaders, and refocus on hungering for their anointing. A hunger for what they have will discourage any proclivity toward criticizing them for who they are not.

I've read the biographies of some of the twentieth century's greatest revivalists, and many of them were eccentric, quirky, or just downright rude. Nevertheless, the Lord enabled them to carry an anointing for a season, and they shaped the course of history.

RESPECTING HIGHER RANKS

Luke chapter 7 recounts Jesus's encounter with a Roman centurion seeking healing for his servant. Jesus decided to respond and started to make His way to the centurion's home. But the centurion stopped Him. He told Jesus, "You don't have to come to my home; just speak the word, and I know my servant will be whole." The centurion explained that he was a man under authority, so he knew Jesus was under His own, higher authority. (See Luke 7:6–7.) What a revelation! The Roman soldier perceived that a key to Jesus's power was His ability to be connected to someone greater.

When I started out as a pastor, I spent a lot of time counseling people in our church. It was part of my job as the assistant pastor of a large congregation. People much older than me would come to my office with major issues that I had never even dreamed of experiencing. I dealt with myriad issues, but what amazed me was the consistency of the wisdom that would flow from my lips. I realized that many of my responses were drawing on the wisdom I had received from my pastors and their apostles. I was actually tapping into a wisdom that preceded me by two generations. Those who sat with me weren't just accessing Troy; they were accessing the wisdom of people twice our age. In short, they were benefitting from a multigenerational anointing.

The Roman centurion in Luke 7 would have been accustomed to giving orders to the soldiers under his command, and to seeing his orders being obeyed. His soldiers obeyed him not just because they respected him but also because his words carried the force of the entire Roman Empire behind them.

Jesus was able to speak with authority to the sickness in the centurion's servant because His words carried the force of God Himself, since Jesus was rightly positioned under God's influence and authority.

Tapping into a greater anointing includes being connected to people who carry a greater anointing. A life connected to people above us gets us access to exponential power. We no longer speak on our own accord, but we begin to carry the force of the person carrying the greater anointing, as well.

Think about a police officer who stands in the middle of a busy street and stops cars weighing ten times as much as he with a simple raising of his hand. He is there to create order and enforce the law. The cars stop because their drivers are responding to the force that the officer's uniform represents. The officer creates order and helps the flow of traffic. But if he removes his uniform and then steps into oncoming traffic, that same officer is killed or injured, or causes a major accident, which, in turn, generates all sorts of traffic problems.

In the church, there are people who have stepped into oncoming traffic, but instead of creating order and helping the flow of things, they create accidents and cause holdups that keep the body of Christ from reaching its proper destination. This is because they are not backed up by anything bigger than themselves. They are out of uniform, and they come across as crazy people playing in the street instead of individuals with real authority.

Of course, many people have problems with this concept because the Western, egalitarian viewpoint wants everything and everyone to be equal. It is true that we all are created equal, and that God isn't a respecter of persons (see Acts 10:34 KJV); but it is also true that there are dimensions of authority that a person may achieve, and we all must remain sensitive enough to recognize and respect that authority.

For example, at a church where I speak on a regular basis, the pastor is younger and less experienced in the ministry than I am. His church is not as large as mine, but none of that matters. When I enter that church, I become the lesser; the pastor is the greater. He is the overseer of that church, and I submit myself to him. If he is not comfortable with a subject that may be on my heart to share with his congregation, I simply refrain from teaching on it, because I am submitted to his authority. Understanding when to submit has created a gateway that has enabled me to receive anointing from those who carry a weightier anointing than mine.

When I find myself in the presence of people of higher-ranking authority, it becomes my joy and honor to receive from them. One of the greatest thrills of my life was to be in the room to witness pastors Ché Ahn and Bill Johnson, two of my biggest influencers, acting like little boys when Dr. David Yonggi Cho laid hands on them and prayed for them. What an amazing sight—two spiritual giants, men of God, becoming completely undone when an apostolic father and incredible general blessed them. Their childlike faith, and their willingness to be blessed by someone greater, are keys to the spiritual authority they possess.

CONTAMINATED LEADERSHIP

Failure is an event, it is not a person.[16]
—*Zig Ziglar*

The other stumbling block I've observed is born from the mistakes of past leaders. Our heavenly Father does have a picture of genuine apostolic leadership, and He doesn't have a problem with the idea of greater rank and greater anointing resting on certain individuals. His heart has always been for genuine biblical expressions of the offices listed in Ephesians 4:11—apostles, prophets, evangelists, pastors, and teachers—to become a reality in the local church. The Father remains committed to these offices, in spite of the periodical failures and falls of those who fulfill these ranks.

When we consider the Father's blueprint for leadership as found in the person of Moses, we see someone who is passionate about the freedom of his people, consumed by the pursuit of justice, willing to share the stage with others for the advancement of a nation, and willing to hear counsel from individuals older and wiser than himself. Yet Moses made mistakes, particularly in the area of anger management.

The church has seen many leaders who were never led in healthy ways. The result has been a style of leadership that reflects the vacant places of their pasts. The church must be careful, however, not to adopt a political spirit that has as its goal "throwing out the bums." God's principle doesn't change, even when there are violations within the application of it. The Lord's heart for His church still includes godly spiritual fathers who can lead His

16. Zig Zigler, *See You at the Top* (Gretna, LA: Pelican Publishing Company, Inc., 1975), 61.

church into renewal experiences and reformations in society. In other words, the Father remains passionate about using men and women of authority in the church, even when some of those individuals let Him down.

> **THE FATHER REMAINS PASSIONATE ABOUT USING MEN AND WOMEN OF AUTHORITY IN THE CHURCH, EVEN WHEN SOME OF THOSE INDIVIDUALS LET HIM DOWN.**

Every gift we receive from the Father has the potential to turn bad when the gift itself becomes the focal point. Unfortunately, many leaders have become the focal point, and have allowed that to happen, instead of refocusing the attention where it belongs—on the Father.

In Acts 12:21–22, King Herod was speaking with such authority that people started shouting, *"The voice of a god and not of a man!"* Immediately, an angel struck down Herod, because, in that moment, Herod refused to give God the glory.

This scriptural drama captures the essence of contaminated headship. It would be impossible for a human body to function without a head, and it is impossible for the body of Christ to perform properly without headship. Thank the Lord that there are leaders throughout the kingdom who aren't self-appointed and who carry the character of God in their lives. The church finds it hard to reject leadership when it embodies character traits that the Lord smiles upon. This type of leadership rejoices in creating environments where others can be successful.

REVELATION CARRIERS

Deuteronomy 17 articulates God's blueprint for leadership by describing what He wants to see in the kings of Israel. It says that the king should be a man carrying revelation, not trapped by materialism, and not willing to manipulate others for his own gain.

Genuine apostolic leadership looks to release revelation into the hearts of the followers, and to cause their perspectives to increase, their functionality to improve.

Bishop Tudor Bismark is a wonderful apostolic father who, along with his wife, Chi-Chi, oversees an extraordinary church in Harare, Zimbabwe. The couple lead a global network of churches, and they have been amazing spiritual parents to me.

On one of my trips to Harare, Bishop Tudor laid hands on me and spoke of the apostolic nature of my ministry. It was the first time I had ever heard such a thing spoken about myself. I vividly remember feeling as if a tuning fork had been struck inside my body, because of how strongly his word and his blessing resonated in my heart.

This is one of the main functions of apostles: They release revelation into the hearts of their listeners, thereby elevating the way those people view themselves. Then, apostles help those people to construct a platform upon which they can fulfill their destiny.

Hanging out with the anointing is such a pivotal practice.

FIGHTING FAMILIARITY

Recently, I had the joy of ministering in the Republic of Botswana for Pastor Marcdonald Ndlovu. Pastor Marcdonald's home is very similar to mine, full of young people with energy who are the future of the ministry and a nation. While there, I shared with them about my early years as a Christian. I told them how important it had been for me, over the years, to access the wisdom of my spiritual fathers. In our egalitarian society, is it easy to buy into the notion that because God loves His children equally, He grants them equal authority.

There was a time, when my natural children were young, that some of my spiritual kids were old enough to drive. I would routinely lend my car to my legally licensed spiritual children, but I never would have even thought about allowing my then-underage natural children to drive, because they weren't legally old enough.

WHEN WE INTERACT WITH A GOD-ORDAINED LEADER, IT IS CRITICAL THAT WE RESIST VIEWING THAT PERSON CASUALLY, AS OFTEN OCCURS WITH INCREASED FAMILIARITY. OTHERWISE, WE WILL TEND TO VIEW THAT PERSON ACCORDING TO THE FLESH INSTEAD OF SEEING HIM OR HER IN THE SPIRIT.

Similarly, in the kingdom, God has some children who are older than we are, spiritually speaking; therefore, they have been given more authority. Our job is to recognize that authority, and not to become offended. Too often, church people dishonor leaders who carry incredible authority in the spirit because they don't have enough discernment to recognize the higher level of authority those leaders carry. Or, even if they do recognize that authority, those people won't allow themselves to give honor where it's due because their own insecurities prohibit them from doing so. It is an easier pill to swallow when one's leader is "just one of the guys." Yet this kind of familiarity is often an obstacle to breakthrough.

When we interact with a God-ordained leader, it is critical that we resist viewing that person casually, as often occurs with increased familiarity. Otherwise, we will tend to view that person according to the flesh instead of seeing him or her in the spirit. I often address this dynamic with my children because I never want them to become so familiar with me that they lose sight of my position in the spirit. I believe this principle is the reason that Eli's sons became wicked. (See 1 Samuel 2:12–36.) They dishonored their father's position in the spirit when they allowed themselves to become too familiar with him and thereby lost respect for the prophet that he was. Consequently, the anointing that should have been their birthright was passed on to a spiritual son of Eli's, named Samuel. The sons of Eli devalued their dad's anointing in their own minds, and it cost them severely.

We must cultivate within our hearts a hunger for what our leaders carry. God has given each of us at least one spiritual leader to whom we should submit. And we will benefit from this relationship to the degree that we value this person, and to the extent that we seek after the spiritual anointing on him or her. At the same time, each of us also has to recognize the particular leadership role God has given to us.

An effective cautionary tale about the dangers of familiarity is the account of Jesus's first public proclamation. In Luke 4:18–19, Jesus announced His mission statement, which was actually the fulfillment of the prophecy recorded in Isaiah 61. In the midst of His declaration, the grace from His words pervaded the room, and His listeners were filled with awe. But then, some people in the crowd realized that the man who was speaking was Jesus, whom they had watched grow up in the home of their neighbor Joseph. (See Luke 4:22.) These people lost sight of the power being released in that moment, and chose to view Jesus merely as the son of a carpenter.

Scripture tells us that from this moment on, Jesus marveled at the people's unbelief, and His hometown of Nazareth became known as a place where the power of God couldn't move. (See Mark 6:4, 6; Luke 4:24.) Instead of living with a sense of wonderment at what Jesus was releasing, these people became snared by their familiarity with Jesus; as a result, they closed an open door that God had provided. They missed the fact that the Messiah they had learned about and had been waiting for was standing in their midst.

Unfortunately, a similar scene plays itself out over and over again in the church today. Many times, we miss out on access points to a greater anointing by stepping over the blessings right in front of us. The maxim "Familiarity breeds contempt" is completely valid. Many people fail to benefit from the anointed leadership God has placed squarely in their path because they think the person is no big deal.

Bishop Timothy Clarke leads a thriving church in Columbus, Ohio. Bishop Clarke is regarded as one of America's best preachers; he is well respected in many circles. However, I've always known Bishop Clarke as "Uncle Tim." His wife was a spiritual daughter of my grandmother, and his mother-in-law was my grandmother's best friend. Uncle Tim has been like family to me for most of my life. He's one of the most gregarious, fun-loving people I know; whenever he's around, he makes me laugh and feel great.

Years ago, the church I was a part of hosted a conference at which he was a guest speaker. Because of our relationship, I had the privilege of greeting Uncle Tim in the green room reserved for conference speakers. We exchanged typical banter, but then I said something—I don't even remember specifically what it was—that went beyond playful banter into the realm of contemptuous familiarity. It wasn't as if my comment was abusive or over the top, but it was just disrespectful enough to indicate that I had lost a sense of the great Christian leader he had become. In that moment, my comment communicated to heaven that I didn't properly regard the anointing on his life. Uncle Tim didn't rebuke me or say anything about it, but when I walked out of that room, I felt sick. I knew I had done something wrong.

Thankfully, the event security staff permitted me to make a quick U-turn and reenter the green room. I pulled Uncle Tim aside, addressed him this time as "Bishop Clarke," and apologized for my disrespectful comment, and for giving myself over to familiarity. I'll never forget his response. I'm paraphrasing, but what he said, in essence, was this: "Troy, I felt the disrespect when you made the comment, but because you knew enough to come back and apologize, not only do I forgive you, I now know how much of a man of God you are and will become."

When we recognize the anointing on a person's life, regardless of how familiar that person may be to us, we communicate to heaven our capacity to receive a measure of what he or she carries.

Admittedly, we've seen grave abuses of power in the church. I'm not suggesting idol worship. We should never lose sight of the humanity of our leaders. But we ought to honor the men and women who speak the Word of God into our lives.

The writer of Hebrews urges us to imitate the faith of those over us in the church. (See Hebrews 13:7, 17.) And the apostle Paul told the church at Corinth to follow him as he followed Christ. (See 1 Corinthians 4:6; 11:1.) It sounds bold and self-serving, but Paul was actually setting Timothy up for breakthrough.

When we are in the presence of a leader who speaks the written Word of God, as well as specific words from God, I believe it is honoring and expedient for us to ask questions about his or her vision—what God is saying, what the person is sensing, and how he or she interprets particular passages of the Bible.

I believe we should engage with, and take genuine interest in, our spiritual leaders. Through these types of exchanges, we'll find God releasing more wisdom to us than we could ever acquire on our own. That type of hunger causes us to grow exponentially in wisdom.

I want to encourage everyone to spend time with their spiritual leaders, engaging them in dialogue and drawing close to them in a healthy way. These practices will result in such blessings when we refuse to allow familiarity to keep us from accessing the deep riches of God that are stored within our leaders, just awaiting our discovery.

IN PRAISE OF APOSTOLIC ALIGNMENT

Earlier in this chapter, I mentioned my three fathers—one biological, two spiritual. It's important to understand that these men have been equally important to me during different phases of my life. Of course, my biological father has always been, and will always be, my father. He is one of the greatest men I've ever known, and it's a blessing that he is the kind of man I can turn to, regardless of the phase of life I'm in. I realize many people don't have the blessing of a godly natural father.

My spiritual fathers, Bishop Thompson and Pastor Ché Ahn, have been equally important to me, which demonstrates a new type of thinking I believe the body of Christ should embrace. In the past, it was common to label relationships between spiritual mentors and their protégés with such phrases as "spiritual covering" or "pastoral covering," yet the connotations have led to many cases of abuse and hurt feelings. It's one of the reasons many people have abandoned this concept altogether. But, in spite of the potential flaws of such an arrangement, a healthy relationship of spiritual mentor/mentee is crucial for growth and advancement.

IN SPITE OF THE POTENTIAL FLAWS OF SUCH AN ARRANGEMENT, A HEALTHY RELATIONSHIP OF SPIRITUAL MENTOR/MENTEE IS CRUCIAL FOR GROWTH AND ADVANCEMENT.

The reality is that life is made of different seasons, each with its own particular needs, and it is not the will of God that one person fulfill all those needs. My life has comprised three distinct seasons, with corresponding needs that were met by three different men, all of them equally important. I shudder to think where I would be if my father wasn't farsighted and mature enough to allow Bishop Thompson to be the primary influence in my life during his particular season.

Perhaps a better phrase for this type of relationship is "apostolic alignment." In Ephesians 4:12, the Greek word *katerismos* is translated as *"equipping"*; a better translation is the term "aligned." The Greek word was actually a medical term referring to the proper setting of bones in the body. We know that when bones get out of alignment, major discomfort occurs. Blood doesn't flow properly, nerves can be pinched—all sorts of negative consequences result when bones are out of alignment. The spirit of what Paul is teaching here is the importance of coming into proper alignment with the teaching and leadership of apostles, prophets, pastors, teachers, and evangelists, so those individuals may perform the works of ministry in a productive way.

Based on the season of life you're in—whether it was initiated by a change in career, church, marital status, neighborhood, or something else—God will bring you into contact with people you ought to align with for that season. Some people may need to make multiple alignments at the same time. One possibility is a tiered alignment system, with a primary alignment as well as secondary and, if needed, tertiary alignments. For example, consider a young woman being mentored by an older single woman who has never been married before. If the young female mentee gets married, she will need to align with someone who can answer some of the specific questions she will have as a married woman. Perhaps, in that season, God will bring into her life a married couple to be her primary mentors. That doesn't mean that her earlier mentor is no longer needed or not relevant; it simply means that she should assume a secondary position of influence, because of her inability to speak into an area of chief concern in the life of her mentee.

This concept is especially important for Christians as they operate in the marketplace. When it comes to the professionals who attend my church, I offer them spiritual counsel and wisdom regarding life skills; I don't, however, presume to provide advice regarding their areas of expertise. For their own professional development, they must select someone else as their primary alignment. I am satisfied to be their secondary or tertiary alignment. It would be foolish of me to think of myself as the only one from whom they should seek advice. Yet within the body of Christ, many souls have been wounded because they were told that their pastoral leader was to be their only overseer.

My grandfather used to say to me, "I need you, and you need me, so let's get along together." Grandpa was right: No man is an island, and no one who has ever done anything significant in life did so without guidance and support.

One of the most important elements of our lives is apostolic alignment. When we're intentional about spending time with people who are further down the road than we are, and when we "hang out" with their anointing, God transfers what they carry onto us, and we accelerate.

When that happens, we see more of the culture of heaven in our midst.

6

PRIVATE LIFE, PUBLIC BREAKTHROUGH

One thing I have observed is this: People who are powerful in public are usually disciplined in private.

In Mark 9, Jesus was confronted by a man who was distraught because none of Jesus's disciples had been able to deliver the man's son from the demon that had plagued him for years. Jesus ministered freedom to the young man. Later, when questioned by His disciples as to why they had not succeeded in ministering deliverance to the boy themselves, Jesus told them that the kind of demon that had plagued that boy comes out only by fasting and prayer. (See Mark 9:29 KJV.) In other words, the disciples didn't have an adequate anointing to confront and expel that particular demon. According to Jesus, the power they lacked in public could be appropriated only by authentic fasting and prayer, done in private. In essence, Jesus told them they would access more power in ministry by cultivating a secret lifestyle of prayer and fasting that was relationship based, not religion based.

What happened in the moment of Jesus's delivering the boy? In that public act, Jesus drew from a reservoir of anointing that He had developed in His private times with God. Jesus had consistently cultivated intimacy with His Father, an intimacy that took precedence over everything else in His life, and it served as the wellspring of power for His public ministry.

God expects us to do the same thing—prioritize intimacy with Him, and treat it not as an optional spiritual discipline that we practice just because we think it's a good idea, but as the very lifeblood of everything we do for the kingdom of heaven.

PRESENCE AND PLACE

> Just as we should breathe air regularly to survive, so we need to pray to live a victorious life.[17]
>
> —*David Yonggi Cho*

On a recent trip to Seoul, Korea, I had a day to myself before our conference began. I love the adventure of international travel, experiencing the culture of the foreign cities I visit. Upon arriving, I exchanged my currency, then took the subway from my hotel to the Yoido part of Seoul. My plan was to attend a morning service at the Yoido Full Gospel Church and, afterward, to catch the church's shuttle to its Osanri Choi Ja-sil Memorial Fasting Prayer Mountain for a time of prayer.

Dr. David Yonggi Cho, who founded Yoido Full Gospel and Prayer Mountain, is rightly regarded as one of the greatest spiritual fathers of our day. Some people change the church; others change the world, and that's what Dr. Cho has done. The Yoido Full Gospel Church is considered to be the largest church in the world, and millions of people have traveled to the Prayer Mountain for fasting and prayer. It is a wonderful place where one strongly senses the presence of God.

---

17. David Yonggi Cho and Wayde Goodall, *Faith: Believing in the God Who Works on Your Behalf* (Racine, WI: BroadStreet Publishing Group, LLC, 2017), 39.

I arrived at Prayer Mountain determined to climb to the top and have a powerful time of prayer before the Lord. When I climbed to the summit, I asked God what I should pray for, and I was led to ask for a fresh infilling of the Holy Spirit. The infilling came, and I was richly blessed. In fact, while in prayer, I began to speak in a new tongue.

Later, as I was coming down the mountain to catch the shuttle back to the city, I was thanking the Lord for the wonderful experience of His presence on this holy Prayer Mountain when, suddenly, I heard God speak to me. He said, "Son, it's no holier than the room where you pray at home." I was rocked. The Father was reminding me that His presence is available to His people wherever they are. I wouldn't dream of minimizing the location of the Prayer Mountain or the encounters with God that thousands of people have had in that place. Yet, that day, I was reminded that presence is far more important than place.

This doesn't mean that place is unimportant. Recently, I toured the Bonnie Brae House in Los Angeles, where, in 1906, William Seymour and his early followers began to pray for the Holy Spirit to fall. Inside the walls of that unassuming house, the Azusa Street Revival began—a revival that swept throughout the world. When I entered the house, the sense of God's presence was so strong that it knocked me over, along with most of the other people with me, and propelled us into a time of great prayer.

WHEREVER WE MEET GOD BECOMES A SANCTIFIED, HOLY PLACE.

Prayer Mountain, and other spiritually notable places, are blessed; but, in Christ, we have the ability to change the atmospheric condition of any geographic location and make it a place where believers will seek God's face and access His manifested presence, just as William Seymour did in a house in Los Angeles, and as Dr. Cho did on a mountain in South Korea. Wherever we meet God becomes a sanctified, holy place.

In the Bible, Jacob fell asleep on a rock in an ordinary place. There was no Tempur-Pedic mattress available to him that night, but God's presence changed an ordinary, unassuming cave into Bethel, the house of God. (See Genesis 28:10–19.) We must always respect the fact that it is God's presence that distinguishes a location and makes it holy. God loves geography.

At the same time, one of the many benefits of the blood of Jesus is that it gives us access to the presence of God wherever we may be. This means that there have been times when my car has become as Bethel; my bathroom has become as Prayer Mountain. Moments spent alone in the secret place with God are sacred and precious to me, for they are the foundation of my public moments with Him.

MILITANCY AND INTIMACY

According to Psalm 103:7, Israel was familiar with the deeds of God, but Moses was familiar with God's ways. This distinction is important. The ways of God may be known only by those who cultivate intimacy with God. Israel—the people of God—had seen many miracles, signs, and wonders, all of them stunning manifestations of God's power. Yet Moses got to know God at a higher level. He not only experienced what God did, he also got to know who God is, and why He does the things He does. What made the difference? In a word, it is *intimacy*.

Early in ministry, I learned to value private moments with God more than times of public encounters with Him. I love meetings where God shows up and reveals His supernatural power. However, I have learned that not every corporate meeting is the same. The degrees of power and anointing vary by gathering. As someone who leads a church, I want every meeting to be great, every offering to be abundant, and every song to be glorious. But those expectations simply aren't realistic. In cultivating intimacy with God by spending secret moments with Him, we train ourselves to have a different focus. As a result, we become able to rest in the intimacy we share with the Father, rather than being driven by a need for visible success in corporate meetings, which, in any case, is difficult to measure due to its innate subjectivity.

I say all this to show how prayer is so much more than we've made it to be. Prayer is, quite simply, fellowship with God. And fellowship with God—intimate communion with the Father—is the healthiest foundation for prayer.

Some people pray by following a pattern; others pray as a means of engaging in spiritual warfare. While these two approaches are certainly important dimensions of a personal prayer life, on their own, they do not make for a sustainable prayer life. I have been involved in ministries that kept up a routine prayer schedule or agendas, and those ministries always seemed to be riddled with inconsistent attendance and sporadic involvement. The problem wasn't the people or the leadership; it was the simple fact that there are times for war and times for peace, and people need rest. If the foundation of our approach to prayer is spiritual warfare, then we will inadvertently associate prayer with warfare, thereby missing out on the fuel of a sustainable prayer life, which is intimate fellowship with the Father.

IF THE FOUNDATION OF OUR APPROACH TO PRAYER IS SPIRITUAL WARFARE, THEN WE WILL INADVERTENTLY ASSOCIATE PRAYER WITH WARFARE, THEREBY MISSING OUT ON THE FUEL OF A SUSTAINABLE PRAYER LIFE, WHICH IS INTIMATE FELLOWSHIP WITH THE FATHER.

To put it another way: Militancy leads to exhaustion, while intimacy leads to elation.

In the human body, the adrenal gland releases the hormone adrenaline into our bodies when we are under stress, such as when we perceive ourselves to be in danger. It is adrenaline that enables men and women to accomplish phenomenal feats of strength in times of crisis. Years ago, a married couple was involved in a car accident. Their car flipped, ejecting the wife. Her husband ended up pinned underneath the vehicle, gasping for breath.

The wife somehow found the strength to get to the car and managed to lift it off her husband, enabling him to roll free to safety. Her fear had created such a boost of adrenaline that it gave her superhuman strength.

Studies by the medical community have taught us that sustained releases of that type of adrenaline can actually harm a person, even unto death. What the doctors tell us is that our bodies are not designed to sustain that type of excitement.

Much of the modern prayer movement is like a sustained shot of adrenaline. We fight devils, pull down strongholds, and storm the gates of hell. All these acts are noble, but if we are not careful, they can prevent us from simply enjoying fellowship with our Father. Many believers start out with noble intentions but end up completely spent, panting for breath on the side of the road.

I became familiar with a church that was witnessing the birth of an exceptional prayer movement. The people met for two hours every morning during the workweek to pray. On Saturdays, they had a two-hour session that included teaching. This church greatly impacted its community with its prayers, and the members performed some remarkable acts of service. However, the church failed to build a sustainable model of prayer for its people because it didn't recognize the reality of seasons. The prayer movement of that church probably reached a peak around 2001. At that time, they had over 75 believers faithfully attending the sessions.

Soon, however, the numbers dropped off, and the momentum and growth seemed to wane. Today, that prayer ministry continues, but it has not returned to the numbers it once enjoyed.

FELLOWSHIP WITH THE FATHER

> To fall in love with God is the greatest of all romances; to seek Him, the greatest adventure; to find him, the greatest human achievement.
>
> —*Augustine*

It is vital that we remember and heed the principle of seasons. Sometimes, the seasons in our lives call for "warfare" prayer, but no one can sustain war indefinitely without rest. Even the nations' militaries know enough to place combat troops on furlough in order to provide the soldiers with renewal and refreshment. Far too few in the church recognize the value of rest, and people are expected to pray at a level that is not sustainable. All this derives from a lack of attentiveness to God's times and seasons.

It is helpful to consider the prayer life of Jesus while He was on earth, because it shows us a balance between times of public confrontation and times of private communion. Jesus had a profoundly inspiring prayer life because it was built primarily on enjoyable fellowship with the Father. Certainly, Jesus confronted devils and pulled down strongholds. Those were moments of great militancy, but they weren't the primary focus of His time. Intimate relationship with the Father was His absolute priority.

Have you ever noticed just how relational the prayer is that Jesus taught to His disciples in Matthew 6? The prayer opens with the words *"Our Father"* (Matthew 6:9), offering us an insight into the way our personal prayer lives should be built. In saying "Our Father," we are confessing the fact that our relationship with God is based on intimacy. That cry, in effect, says this: "God, I know

You are the supreme being of heaven and earth, but You are also my loving daddy." Before we even begin to pray *"Your kingdom come"* (Matthew 6:10) or *"Deliver us from evil"* (Matthew 6:13), we say, "Our Daddy in the heavens!" That should give us a clue as to what our priority should be!

We are God's children, and so our spirits, according to the apostle Paul, call out to God, saying, *"Abba! Father!"* (Romans 8:15). In Jewish family life, the term "Abba" connotes intimacy between a father and his child. In the Christian context, the word points to the closeness we as New Testament believers enjoy with Father God.

In John 15:7, Jesus told His disciples that if they abided in Him, they could ask for whatever they wanted, and it would be granted to them. In essence, He was saying that intimacy is directly correlated to productivity. The deeper our intimacy with the Father, the greater our productivity for the Father will be. That's a mighty equation!

> **JESUS TOLD HIS DISCIPLES THAT IF THEY ABIDED IN HIM, THEY COULD ASK FOR WHATEVER THEY WANTED, AND IT WOULD BE GRANTED TO THEM. IN ESSENCE, HE WAS SAYING THAT INTIMACY IS DIRECTLY CORRELATED TO PRODUCTIVITY.**

The world teaches that in order to achieve great things, we have to work hard, strive, and step over our mothers to get up the corporate ladder. In the kingdom of heaven, however, these ideas get turned on their head. In John 15:7, we learn a new way. Jesus effectively says, "If you'll just hang close to Daddy God, then you'll achieve all that you ever wanted, and beyond." What a liberating concept! In our culture, people are getting worn out by the notion that they must grind out some type of living, let alone significance.

But, over 2,000 years ago, Jesus shared with us a revolutionary key. He taught that all we needed to do was hang out with our Father God, and we would see productivity and abundance in our lives. The key is resting in Him and remaining in Him; it is simply having fellowship with Him.

The only time Jesus "labored in prayer" was in the garden of Gethsemane, because of the weighty task in front of Him, and the foreboding sense that His fellowship with the Father was about to be broken. According to the gospels of Matthew and Mark, Jesus never said a word during the crucifixion experience until His fellowship with the Father was broken. Then He cried out with a loud voice, *"My God, My God, why have You forsaken me?"* (Matthew 27:46; Mark 15:34). Jesus remained silent throughout the most horrific beatings and torture imaginable. While people ridiculed and cursed Him, He never defended Himself or said anything about the pain He was experiencing. Yet His fellowship with the Father was so crucial that when it was broken, it caused Jesus to scream.

Psalm 51 records David as crying out to God, "Please don't take Your Spirit from me." (See Psalm 51:11.) In other words, "Don't let our close fellowship be fractured." Prayer certainly encompasses seasons of war and petition, but prayer must always have its moorings in the fellowship, love, and intimacy that God desires to have with His people.

DESPERATE, NOT DESTITUTE

> The irony is that while God doesn't need us but still wants us, we desperately need God but don't really want Him most of the time.[18]
>
> —*Francis Chan*

18. Francis Chan, *Crazy Love* (Colorado Springs, CO: David C. Cook, 2008), 59.

I recently had a conversation with a man in my congregation who told me he believed his life had been in a downward spiral ever since a traumatic event he had experienced a few years back. After patiently listening to his lament, I finally broke in and said, "Gee, that's funny. I see your life as quite the opposite. I think you've been getting better and better since that time." Since I have been his pastor for a number of years, I was able to give him an overall rundown of all the things that had happened to him since the traumatic event to which he was referring.

We talked about his strengthened relationship with his wife, the birth of their first child, his financial stability throughout the recession, his improved health, and his ministry opportunities. By the time I was done, he was repenting (in the literal sense of changing his thinking), because he had come to realize how good God had been to him through the years. What's more, he also realized that since the initial trauma, he had made several mistakes, yet God had still been good to him.

At the end of our talk, this gentleman understood that he had been making judgments about his life and his God based on a brief period of time. It reminded me of just how myopic and tunnel-minded our society can be. This fact isn't entirely our own fault, of course. Developments in technology over the last ten years have created a world where we can do many things instantly. I believe this culture of instant gratification has undermined our ability to rely and live dependent on the Father.

Part of the prayer Jesus taught to His disciples, as recorded in Matthew 6:9–13, is a request for *"our daily bread"* (Matthew 6:11). I once asked the Father why He wants us praying for daily bread when He has identified Himself as Jehovah-Jireh, which means "the God of provision." He said, "Son, I don't want you destitute, but I do want you desperate." This response gave me a great a key to understanding His mind. Prayer helps us to maintain a hunger for God that connects us to Him in such a way that we are changed from the inside out.

Prayer is therefore vital for finding and keeping the presence of God and for bringing the culture of heaven to earth. Prayer is a radical act that actually changes the world. It brings heaven to earth, transforming the people and places where God's kingdom invades in response to our heartfelt prayers.

If this is so, then why don't more Christians spend more time in prayer? The answer is that one of Satan's strategies has been to rob people of the joy of prayer.

Jesus taught that answered prayers provoke fullness of joy in our hearts. Consider this passage from the gospel of John:

> [Jesus said,] *"In that day you will not question Me about anything. Truly, truly, I say to you, if you ask the Father for anything in My name, He will give it to you. Until now you have asked for nothing in My name; ask and you will receive, so that your joy may be made full."* (John 16:23–24)

Prayer, while often laborious, should be a joyous practice. Yet many people stop praying because they don't experience the joy that they are supposed to derive from it. Many Christians pray only because they feel it is the "Christian" thing to do. They may engage in prayer as a discipline, but even the most disciplined among us cannot sustain a consistent prayer life in the name of piety.

THE SEED PRINCIPLE

One reason prayer can become laborious is that we tend to lack discernment regarding when we have been called to press in for something and when we have already received something and ought to back off from prayer so we may celebrate our victory, instead.

In one sense, every prayer is always answered. We have this assurance from the apostle John:

> *These things I have written to you who believe in the name of the Son of God, so that you may know that you have eternal life. This is the confidence which we have before Him, that, if we ask anything according to His will, He hears us. And if we know that He hears us in whatever we ask, we know that we have the requests which we have asked of Him.*
>
> (1 John 5:13–15)

In this passage, John explains that if God hears us, then we can be assured that we have received that which we have asked for. Why, then, do people keep praying for the things that God's Word says they already have? It's because most people don't understand the principle of the seed. Every prayer we release that falls in sync with God's will for our lives is answered, most of the time in "seed" form. At that point, our job is to recognize the seed and to start the process of cultivation. Mark 4:28 says, "*The soil produces crops by itself; first the blade, then the head, then the mature grain in the head.*" In the process of growth, the seed comes first, followed by the first blade and, finally, the fully developed plant. Most people walk right past the fact that God answered their prayer because the answer was given in seed form; consequently, instead of stopping to cultivate the seed into something tangible, they keep "plowing the field" in prayer for months, becoming more and more frustrated in the process because they were expecting God to give them the fully developed plant right away.

From time to time, we are all guilty of missing the seed. When this happens, it is detrimental to our prayer life. We may continue dutifully in prayer, but we experience no joy, because, in our mind, we haven't received what we've been asking for.

Sometimes, the problem is as simple as our difficulty in believing God has answered our prayers. Once, on a ministry trip, I was assigned an assistant for the week from the host church. En route to one of the meetings, I engaged this young lady in conversation about her hopes and desires. She shared some things with me and then asked for my opinion. I gave her a few suggestions, and she quickly responded, "I'll have to pray about that." I have probably heard that response a thousand times. While the comment can be legitimate, in some people, it is an indication of disbelief—a refusal to entertain the idea that they may have just received their answer in the counsel that was heard. The tendency is to drop back into the ritual of praying because it feels safer to do that than to move forward in faith. Instead of taking a stand in faith and believing that they've received their answer, they will go back into their prayer closet. Instead of going into the rarefied air of faith, where one dismisses anxiety, recognizes the seed, and starts building on it, they reckon it's far less risky to remain in unbelief and return for more prayer.

At one point or another, most of us fall into this trap because our minds are still in the process of being renewed (see Romans 12:2); we're still learning to see invisible things with greater clarity than visible things.

When I was leading a team of church planters, I was praying about establishing that ministry in three or four cities, and I took a trip to Richmond, Virginia—one of the cities we were considering—for a time of prayer and fasting. One day, I went to a park in the city called Church Hill, sat on one of the benches, and began to ask God, "Where do You want me to go?" I heard the Lord say back to me, "Son, I'm with you wherever you go. Where do you want to go?" I was shocked by His response, but I answered Him, "I want to go to Providence." He said, "Well then, go to Providence!"

In that moment, I had a choice. I could either rejoice that God had given me my heart's desires, or I could say, "Lord, I need to pray about this some more." Had I chosen the latter, I would have missed my answer because of hidden unbelief. Thankfully, I made the right choice! The time for prayer was over; it was now time to step out on faith, to make decrees that were aligned with God's answer to me, and to start cultivating the seed He had released.

Proverbs 13:12 says, *"Hope deferred makes the heart sick, but desire fulfilled is a tree of life."* Many people experience moments like mine and choose the wrong response. They enter into an endless cycle of praying and praying for something they have already received, and they end up heartsick because they failed to recognize that the answer came in the form of a seed that was destined and designed to grow into a tree of life. Always remember: A prayer life that is marked by answers and not just hours is a joyous prayer life. It's a model of prayer that we'll come back to, again and again.

A PRAYER LIFE THAT IS MARKED BY ANSWERS AND NOT JUST HOURS IS A JOYOUS PRAYER LIFE. IT'S A MODEL OF PRAYER THAT WE'LL COME BACK TO, AGAIN AND AGAIN.

I still remember the first day we walked into our newly renovated church building. The work was not yet completed: There was no carpet, and yellow tape was strung to keep people out of the active construction zones. During our first meeting, the local fire marshal stood vigilantly in the back of the room, watching to ensure we weren't violating any of his codes.

The day before the first meeting, sawdust covered every surface. Many of the members came out to help us clean. We cleaned all night long. But even though the place looked like a wreck, that first Sunday was a joyous day for our church family, because it was a seed of what we had prayed for.

It is in that realm that Jesus wants us to live. Jesus wants us to understand and experience the inseparable connection between joy and prayer.

PRAYING WITH GOD

> To have God speak to the heart is a majestic experience, an experience that people may miss if they monopolize the conversation and never pause to hear God's responses.[19]
>
> —*Charles Stanely*

One of the most important keys to experiencing joy in prayer is to understand the principle of collaboration. In other words, we mustn't just pray *to* God; we must pray *with* God.

The Holy Spirit loves to speak to us and give us His view on things. There was a popular song I used to sing in which one of the verses is a request for God to give us vision—to help us see things the way He sees them. Many times, we become frustrated in our prayer life because we're praying to God instead of praying with God. Learning to jettison our perspective on a matter, and to opt for God's perspective, instead, is a key to praying with Him. It's crucial that we ask God to give us His view of the person or circumstance we're praying about. I've had to ask God again and again to remind me of how He views my city, because it is easy to slip into soulish prayers, which originate in our feelings—feelings that are often made negative by the distressing circumstances we observe. Whenever I realize that my prayers are soulish, I deliberately switch from soul to spirit, and I rediscover the refreshment of God's perspective.

Many a prayer life has been shipwrecked because too much time was spent praying from an earthly perspective of depression and fear. God has a vision for the people and issues in our lives, and His vision is always one of goodness, one of hope, one where He'll show us what can be, as opposed to what is. When we learn to pray

19. Charles F. Stanley, *How to Listen to God* (Nashville, TN: Thomas Nelson, 1985), 94.

in sync with His view on things, prayer becomes a refreshing part of our lives.

> **CHOOSING TO VIEW THINGS FROM GOD'S PERSPECTIVE, EVEN IN THE DARKEST OF SITUATIONS, WILL PUT A SMILE ON OUR FACES, THEREBY ENABLING US TO HEAR HIS VOICE WITH GREATER CLARITY AND AT A LOUDER VOLUME.**

I was listening to something on my iPhone that made me smile, and I noticed that the upward movement of my jaw caused the earbuds to become wedged more snugly in my ears, which, in turn, resulted in a major improvement of the sound quality. I started experimenting, alternately smiling and frowning to test the difference. Every time I frowned, the sound seemed further away, and the earbuds became loosened, to the point of falling out. The act of smiling activated certain muscles that caused my hearing ability to improve. The reality is, when you are smiling, you can hear better—and that applies to hearing from God, too. Choosing to view things from God's perspective, even in the darkest of situations, will put a smile on our faces, thereby enabling us to hear His voice with greater clarity and at a louder volume.

My issue with many so-called prayer warriors and intercessors is that they spend countless hours praying in reaction to what Satan has done, as opposed to praying in response to what God has said. Those people don't last long as prayer warriors, and they often become embittered, because they're constantly bombarding the gates of hell instead of exploring the halls of heaven.

Believers spend entirely too much time and energy on Satan. It's amazing to me how much research is done on matters related to the demonic realm, and how much time and energy we give to Satan. Satan is not God's equal; he is not the yin to God's yang.

Yet many people spend entirely too much time focused on the activities of hell. They become unbalanced in their personal lives, and some become ineffective Christians, casualties of war.

Jesus never went chasing demons; He only dealt with the ones that got in His way. I won't deny that we need to be knowledgeable about spiritual warfare and dealing with satanic activity, but that knowledge should not exceed our familiarity with what God is saying. I want my prayer life to be dominated by what heaven is saying, not by what Satan is doing.

KNOCKING ON HEAVEN'S DOOR

I like how the *New Living Translation* renders Jesus's statement in Luke 11:9: *"And so I tell you, keep on asking, and you will receive what you ask for. Keep on seeking, and you will find. Keep on knocking, and the door will be opened to you."*

There's a persistence that we must have in our prayer lives. When we pray, the Bible tells us, we shouldn't ask just once but should keep on asking. This idea sounds counterintuitive, especially when juxtaposed against the concept of declaring in faith and not having to ask for things any longer. But the excitement of prayer is learning to work with the Holy Spirit in various ways. In some instances, God leads us to ask once, in faith; to believe we've received our request; and to thank Him for the breakthrough. In other instances, we're led to go on asking—to keep on pushing against that boulder until we see it move.

There are moments when we ought to persist in bombarding the gates of heaven. On such occasions, it's good to know God's heart, to know that what we're persistently praying for is His will. Then, we can put Him in remembrance of His own word about the situation.

The gospel of Luke records what happened when, after a night of unsuccessful fishing, Simon Peter received this instruction from Jesus: *"Put out into the deep water and let down your nets for a catch*" (Luke 5:4). Simon Peter's response should be the posture we assume in seasons of persistent prayer: "Lord, we've been fishing all night, and we haven't caught anything. But because You say so, I'll cast out my net again." (See Luke 5:5.) The passage goes on to tell us that Simon Peter pulled in such a load of fish that his nets began to break, and he had to enlist some friends to help him haul in his catch. (See Luke 5:6–7.) Simon Peter was wise enough to give it one more try because it was Jesus who had told him that this was the thing to do. We need to be able to keep praying when Jesus has told us that the breakthrough will come if we'll just give it one more try.

I sometimes find myself crying out to God to remember His word to me. I'll say, "Lord, wait a minute. You're the one who said that such and such a thing would happen, so I know this is Your desire. I didn't bring it up; You did, so I'll keep pressing in until the breakthrough comes." Whether we're praying for the salvation of a loved one, the success of a business, a financial breakthrough, a new ministry, a fresh anointing, or something else, it is important to remain persistent. Because of our persistence, an internal infrastructure develops within us that gives us the load-bearing capacity we will need to carry the weight of everything God wants to release to us.

WHETHER WE'RE PRAYING FOR THE SALVATION OF A LOVED ONE, THE SUCCESS OF A BUSINESS, A FINANCIAL BREAKTHROUGH, A NEW MINISTRY, A FRESH ANOINTING, OR SOMETHING ELSE, IT IS IMPORTANT TO REMAIN PERSISTENT.

Persistence in prayer prepares our hearts and paves the way to the place where God can do exceeding, abundantly more than we ask or imagine. (See Ephesians 3:20.) There are places of dominion the Lord has for us that, if He were to give them to us in our current internal state, would harm or hinder us rather than bless us. So, He invites us into the process of persistent prayer, where we have to pray through till we see victory. That process beckons us to keep asking, seeking, and knocking. (See Matthew 7:7–8.) Weeks and months may pass as this divinely ordained process develops strength within us so that even in times of disappointment, we simply won't quit.

Most people pray for something once and then give up if they don't get that thing the very next day. But persistence in prayer will cause us to keep asking God because we have a promise from Him that has become our target and our fuel. Through our persistent pursuit, God develops an internal mechanism so strong that, when He releases everything He has for us, we have the load-bearing capacity to not only stand up under it but also be a channel of that blessing to others.

PRAYER AND PERSISTENCE

Storm the throne of grace and persevere therein,
and mercy will come down.
—*John Wesley*

Persistence in prayer is vital, not only for finding solutions to simple needs but also for unlocking the door to our hopes and dreams.

In Luke 18, Jesus shared a parable with His disciples to illustrate *"that at all times they ought to pray and not to lose heart"* (verse 1):

> *"In a certain city there was a judge who did not fear God and did not respect man. There was a widow in that city, and she kept coming to him, saying, 'Give me legal protection from*

> *my opponent.' For a while he was unwilling; but afterward he said to himself, 'Even though I do not fear God nor respect man, yet because this widow bothers me, I will give her legal protection, otherwise by continually coming she will wear me out.'" And the Lord said, "Hear what the unrighteous judge said; now, will not God bring about justice for His elect who cry to Him day and night, and will He delay long over them? I tell you that He will bring about justice for them quickly. However, when the Son of Man comes, will He find faith on the earth?"* (Luke 18:2–8)

This parable reveals so much about the Father, particularly His righteousness. Two important consequences flow out of that character trait. First, we learn that God is concerned about righting the wrongs in our world. So many people have suffered injustices at the hands of others or by satanic forces, and it's good news that God is concerned about straightening out those situations. Second, Jesus says that God is going to bring justice without delay. God wants to accelerate the time of our recompense. The big challenge we must meet is carrying the type of faith that enables us to persist in praying for something, even when we don't see it coming to pass right away. Will He find that kind of faith in the earth?

THE BIG CHALLENGE WE MUST MEET IS CARRYING THE TYPE OF FAITH THAT ENABLES US TO PERSIST IN PRAYING FOR SOMETHING, EVEN WHEN WE DON'T SEE IT COMING TO PASS RIGHT AWAY.

PRAYER AND PASSION

Many people have rightly called prayer a spiritual discipline, but I believe prayer can transcend the realm of discipline. We can transition from a place where we ought to pray to a place where we long to pray.

I once heard Bill Johnson say, "Christianity was never supposed to be known by its disciplines; it was always supposed to be known by its passions." These passions ought to include our prayer lives. But how does this happen?

Passion in prayer develops through thanksgiving and praise. In the Old Testament—under the old covenant—God told Moses that His people would be *"a kingdom of priests…"* (Exodus 19:6). Every believer is a priest, and the primary job of a priest, under the new covenant, is to minister to the Lord through fragrant offerings of worship.

When I first became a Christian, I spent all my prayer time asking for things. I soon learned that the greater position to take in my private time with God was a posture of worship. Worship calls forth God's tangible presence, and that presence makes praying easier and more profound. In His presence, we start to see the things that are of concern to us in the same way God sees them, and this new perspective changes the way we pray. Moreover, in His presence, our affections toward Him grow. All that begins with thanksgiving and praise.

In a healthy marriage, a husband and wife grow more and more in love with each other as the years pass. No husband who loves his wife has to be told to discipline himself to spend time with her. No one ever has to coerce him, or plead with him, or get him to sign up on a chart, to spend time with his wife. He never has to build himself up before taking his wife out on a date. The very thought of having to work hard to spend time with his wife is absurd, because a husband's passion for his wife should always be more than enough fuel to motivate him to be with her.

The Father wants this type of devotion from us. He doesn't want our discipline. He'll take discipline, but discipline will always be less sustainable than, and inferior to, passion. For this reason, it is critical that we add to the realms of our servanthood and soldiering the identity of true sonship. As Mike Bickle, leader of the International House of Prayer, has said, "There are lovers, and there are workers; and lovers always get more done." Sons are lovers. Sons just love their dads.

When my son was younger and still lived at home, he and I loved spending time together. It was never a difficult thing for me to say to him, "Troy, let's go to the movies." He would jump right in the car, and we'd have a great time. That's what the Lord does: He's always calling for us, always asking us to spend time with Him. He continuously beckons us into deeper, more meaningful relationship.

Viewing prayer strictly as a discipline can create a mental blockage that hinders the people of God from spending passion-filled time with their heavenly Father. Don't get me wrong; discipline is an important element to fall back on when the passion simply isn't there. But treating prayer as a discipline alone is just not sustainable. Discipline doesn't have the internal, self-starting fuel of true passion. When prayer is reduced to being viewed as a discipline, it is robbed of the joy that should come from simple communion with God. Instead, prayer becomes a chore, a task, or an accomplishment, as opposed to fellowship.

WHEN PRAYER IS REDUCED TO BEING VIEWED AS A DISCIPLINE, IT IS ROBBED OF THE JOY THAT SHOULD COME FROM SIMPLE COMMUNION WITH GOD. INSTEAD, PRAYER BECOMES A CHORE, A TASK, OR AN ACCOMPLISHMENT, AS OPPOSED TO FELLOWSHIP.

Many people soldier on in prayer instead of embracing the chance to spend time with the most loving Father. Certainly, there are seasons for spiritual warfare—times when we do have to enter into spiritual battle, or exercise pure discipline in order to pray about certain subjects or events. I would never suggest that the need for intercessory warfare or other spiritual disciplines has passed away. But even those disciplines can be infused with the confidence and joy that result from passionate exchanges between the Father and us, His children. This makes Jesus's charge in Luke 18:1 that people ought to always pray much more palatable. When prayer and passion are connected, the restrictions are lifted. There is less of a need for "set" times of prayer. We find ourselves running to God's throne room, our heart and our flesh aching for the presence of the Lord. (See Psalm 84.)

All day, every day, is a good time to pray.

PRAYER AND POWER

When I was a college student, like many other males my age, I opted to invest in a great stereo system rather than spend my money on "less important" things, such as food. I may have been starving, but at least my music sounded great. The keys to my stereo system were a subwoofer, designed to produce deep, rich bass sounds, and a receiver that had enough power to make the subwoofer work properly. That combination made my jazz collection sound amazing. When I moved to Boston, a friend who heard my stereo figured that by purchasing the same subwoofer, he could replicate the same sound with his own stereo. The problem was that his stereo's receiver didn't have enough power to make the subwoofer perform properly. I remember how disappointed he was when we hooked up his new subwoofer, turned on the power, and heard a sound that reminded us of a transistor radio from the sixties. The receiver had cool lights and lead indicators; it sat in a nice rack, but it couldn't make the subwoofer speaker produce the rich sound it was built for because it didn't have enough power.

Many people in the church are like my friend's stereo. They have the greatest equipment and the coolest-looking components; but, lacking power, they can't produce. This power they're missing is the anointing of God flowing through their lives. It is the presence and power of the Holy Spirit that guides us into all truth and leads us to do things we can't even imagine.

As a kid, I loved the superheroes Superman and Spiderman. One moment, they were seemingly regular members of society; the next moment, they sensed a need and leapt into action, being transformed in the process. These guys always showed up to defend people against evil and to set things right using supernatural means.

In Christ, we get to be the superheroes. His anointing rests on us; but, unlike Superman and Spiderman, we aren't trying to hide our true identity. Rather, we want the world to get to know Christ through us.

God's anointing flowing through us is the most important element needed for us to faithfully fulfill the mandate on our lives. The anointing of God is precious. Scholars say that the oil used in Solomon's temple went through seven pressings in order to be made as pure as possible. It was precious then, and it remains our most valuable commodity.

WE JOURNEY INTO DEEPER AND DEEPER REALMS OF THE ANOINTING AS WE LIVE WITH A HUNGER FOR GOD.

There are so many mysteries about God's anointing that we could spend an entire lifetime discovering them. I believe we journey into deeper and deeper realms of the anointing as we live with a hunger for God. The good news is, there is always more of the anointing available. God is always releasing fresh dimensions, and the more we seek Him, the more aspects of Him we discover. In all this, we don't know exactly what we're doing; indeed, we would never presume to be "experts" on the anointing. The moment we think we've mastered the anointing is the moment we lose it. We must aggressively protect our voracious hunger and childlike sense of wonder.

I have learned to cherish a childlike sense of wonder, because I have found it attracts more of God. I never want to be complacent, for complacency leads to routine and a sense of familiarity, which breed contempt for God in the life of the believer. Truthfully, the cancer in so many believers is a sense of routine and expertise; they are unimpressed, always sporting a "been there, done that" attitude. It's time to become childlike again, because what we receive in exchange is supernatural! Let's fight against becoming so dominated by the five senses that we lose sight of the awesome nature of living in God's presence.

Jesus told His disciples not to prevent the children from coming to Him, because the kingdom of God belongs to those who adopt the posture of a playful, trusting child. (See Matthew 19:14; Luke 18:16.) The will of the Father is for His children to freely run and jump on His lap, kiss His face, gaze at Him in wonder, and experience His presence and touch. He rejects the proud but gives grace to the humble. (See James 4:6.) Children don't have a prideful sense of self; they just love freely and walk with a sense of wonder. They are amazed at everything. And that's how we ought to be when it comes to God.

PRIVATE TIMES AND POWER TIMES

When my daughter, Maya, was young, she would squeal with glee whenever I walked in the door of our home. To this day, she is an absolute "Daddy's girl." One of the things Maya and I used to do was lie down together and watch *SportsCenter* on ESPN. Maya had no interest whatsoever in sports—she preferred playing dress-up with dolls—but she would watch that show with me because, for her, it wasn't about ESPN; it was about spending time with her dad.

We talked earlier of the account in Mark 9 in which Jesus delivered a young man of a demon that was affected only by prayer and fasting. However, Jesus didn't stop to pray or fast before He drove out the demon. So, what did He mean? Jesus was referring to prayers He had prayed well in advance of being confronted with this young man's need. In essence, He was accessing the power of God based on an intimacy He had cultivated with His Father when no one was looking, while there was no pressure on Him to minister.

This story teaches us one the most valuable lessons about the anointing: Going after the anointing in order to do something specific is not the best motive. Our heavenly Father desires relationship with His kids without any strings attached. Remember what I shared about my daughter's watching ESPN with me? Maya didn't care at all about the latest basketball trades or golf scores; all she cared about was hanging out with her father. She wasn't out to get something from me; she simply loved spending time with her dad. Even though she's much older now, she still enjoys spending time together watching sports. What fascinates me is that, because of the time we've spent together, Maya has gained a greater sense of what is important to me, and of the way I think. She has also grown in her trust of me. Those things became by-products of the time we spent together doing nothing more than watching ESPN.

When we live in awe of God, in love with His presence, His anointing and power come to us as a simple overflow of time spent with the Father.

In this way, our private times become our power times.

7

HAVE A DRINK ON US!

All Christians experience seasons of needing to leave their usual church environment in order to receive a drink of living water from another source. Every local body of believers has its own "water" that carries a unique flavor, and no church's water carries all flavors. Sometimes, the "flavor" of living water I need from God must be found in a different church or gathering from the one I typically attend.

One of my favorite "watering" holes is Bethel Church in Redding, California. The DNA of that church and its heavenly culture is precious to me; whenever I go there, I leave feeling refreshed, inspired, and revived, sensing greater revelation about what the Father is doing.

Redding is not a large city; thus, getting there requires some effort. Yet countless people flock to Bethel Church to receive an impartation, a healing, a touch from God. To hear the senior pastor, Bill Johnson, list all the countries represented at any given Sunday service is like listening to a roll call from a United Nations meeting. People converge on Bethel because they recognize it as a place to get blasted once again by the Holy Spirit. It is a premier "spring" with living water flowing out of it. I take drinks frequently at Bethel Church.

In Ephesians 5:18, Paul says that believers are to be filled with the Holy Spirit. The best translation of the original Greek text is as follows: "Go on being filled with the Holy Spirit again and again and again." Every believer needs continual replenishment.

You may have heard the story of the great nineteenth-century preacher D. L. Moody's preaching about being "filled" again and again with the Holy Spirit. A little old lady in the front row asked him, "Why do you talk about being 'filled' again and again?" Moody looked directly at her and replied, "Madam, because I leak!"

We all need times of refreshment and replenishment. We all need seasons when God gives us fresh outpourings of His Spirit. Life has a way of taking energy from us, so it becomes critical to take a drink of the Holy Spirit every chance we get, in a place where the atmosphere is filled with heaven—where the culture of heaven has infused and transformed the cultures of earth.

**LIFE HAS A WAY OF TAKING ENERGY FROM US,
SO IT BECOMES CRITICAL TO TAKE A DRINK OF THE HOLY SPIRIT
EVERY CHANCE WE GET.**

This truth shows us the importance of spiritual atmosphere. Jesus could do no mighty works in His hometown of Nazareth because the atmosphere was too full of unbelief. (See Matthew 13:58; Mark 6:6.) The environment was simply not conducive to God's power operating at maximum capacity.

Picture this: Jesus, the Son of God, never missed the mark. He was always in tune with the Father, and He understood atmospheres; yet even His anointing was subject to His spiritual environment.

The environments we expose ourselves to can bring life or death. When I travel to Los Angeles, I am always amazed at how visible the smog is. Some days, there seems to be a gray cloud hovering over the city, and seeing it reminds me of the atmospheres of unbelief that sit over the lives of so many people. Satan works to create and sustain that cloud of unbelief through disappointments and failures.

When it feels as if the cloud over your life is thickening, you may require a change of environment to give you a fresh perspective. Spiritual atmosphere is critical because it has the power to determine how much of God a person will experience.

I know that we live under an open heaven, wherever we are, and that part of our dominion includes controlling and setting atmospheres through prophetic declarations and worship. Even so, it is refreshing to be able to join with other believers and jump into an atmosphere of faith where it isn't necessary to work so hard to create momentum.

BEING MADE NEW

In 1 Samuel 10, Saul received a prophetic word from the prophet Samuel. He encountered a group of prophets who were worshipping the Lord and prophesying. As they got nearer to Saul, suddenly, he began to prophesy as well, and the Scriptures say he was changed into another man. (See 1 Samuel 10:6.) The atmosphere was so pregnant with fire and faith that Saul started moving in the power of God and, more importantly, was changed in his inner man. Unfortunately for Saul, he didn't continue to cultivate what God had started in him, and he eventually buckled to the fear of man.

You and I must go beyond Saul and drink in the Spirit of God on a continual basis, as Paul talked about in Ephesians 5:18. The practice of taking continual drinks of God's power keeps that power flowing into us. We want that power to be flowing out of us as well, resulting in ministry that changes nations. However, we must remember the other benefit: We are made new. Our thinking is transformed, our fears disappear, our old habits die, and we become more like Jesus.

I drink from the river of God all the time, and my drinking often takes me to different geographic places where I know the atmosphere is conducive to my inner spiritual growth. When we go to these places to get filled and refreshed, God increases the measure of power we carry, and changes us. Oftentimes, we desire more power and greater anointing, but we miss the change God wants to bring to our hearts.

It's like popping the hood on a big American muscle car from the sixties, only to find that the motor is from a kid's scooter. The car looks strong on the outside, but it has no horsepower on the inside. Too many leaders and churches are so fixated on their outward development that they lose sight of the inner power and authority they've been granted. Their ministries look strong on the surface because of the numbers of people who come to the church, lives that are changed, and signs and wonders that occur. But when someone pops open the hood, it becomes clear that the church or leader cannot sustain the move of God with which it has been graced. Throughout church history, this process has happened again and again. That is why God is looking for a people, a leader, a church, that will pay the price for revival.

> **AN INCREASE IN OUR MEASURE OF ANOINTING AND POWER IS NOT MERELY FOR OUR MINISTRY TO OTHERS;**
> **IT COMES TO CHANGE OUR VERY HEARTS, AND TO TRANSFORM US INTO PEOPLE WHO LOOK MORE LIKE JESUS.**

It's important to remember that an increase in our measure of anointing and power is not merely for our ministry to others; it comes to change our very hearts, and to transform us into people who look more like Jesus. Many powerful men and women have not finished well. The power working through their lives influenced what they did, but they stopped short of allowing that power to influence who they were. Jesus said to His disciples, "I have much more to share with you, more than you can bear." (See John 16:12.) He recognized that His disciples wouldn't have the load-bearing capacity for what He wanted to tell them until the Holy Spirit came.

Increasing in our measure of the anointing gives us power to do greater works. It also gives us the internal structure necessary to sustain all that God wants to release into our lives.

CHASING AFTER GOD

> Don't limit God to fit in the way that you think that He is going to speak, because just about the time that we think we have Him figured out, He will oftentimes speak to us in another way.[20]
>
> —*Randy Clark*

No one has the market cornered on revelation. Some of the greatest elements of our ministry at home have come from things we've seen other churches doing and from impartations we've received from other places. Conferences can provide us with helpful information, but the Father is looking to grant us an impartation. In other words, He doesn't just want to fill our heads; it is the Father's good pleasure to fill our hearts.

In 2009, I attended the Voice of the Apostles Conference in Baltimore, hosted by Randy Clark and his ministry, Global Awakening. Prior to leaving for Baltimore, I told a friend I felt as

20. Randy Clark, *Words of Knowledge* (Mechanicsburg, PA: Global Awakening, 2001), 37.

if God was going to do something special for me during the conference. Back in 2008, I had begun asking God to give me more of Him. I had heard testimonies from people who had gone to Toronto during the great revival of the nineties—a revival that is still going on today—and had been touched beautifully by God. I had heard of people getting blasted by God at Harvest Rock Church in Pasadena, California, and at Brownsville Assemblies of God in Pensacola, Florida. All these stories increased my longing for a similar experience with God. I yearned to be touched in a profound way, so I started praying in the style in which I had heard that the others had prayed. I simply asked God to give me more.

I prayed for months. People around me started getting touched, but it still wasn't happening to me. I honestly started to wonder if I would ever receive a touch from God such as I had envisioned. I reasoned that I had no right to dictate the terms of His touch, which was true; yet I was still hungry. I then began to think maybe I should just celebrate what I had been receiving from God, even though it didn't look the way I thought it would. Yet I was still hungry. When it was time for the Voice of the Apostles Conference, I had been praying and hungering for an experience with God for well over a year. Some nights, I would go to sleep saying, "More, Lord." It became a cry in my heart that was almost on autopilot.

The first nights of the conference were wonderful. Pastor Bill Johnson was one of the speakers, and he gave a word of knowledge about neuropathy in the body. He then had us pray for people who needed a miracle in this area. I laid hands on a woman whose neuropathy had caused her toes to remain permanently curled. She was unable to flatten her feet, and the act of walking caused her severe pain, so she had to do so very gingerly. She also needed to wear special shoes. I had her take off her shoes, and as she prayed according to my guidance, her toes straightened out; for the first time in many months, she walked flat-footed—all the way to the stage to give her testimony. Her friends were overjoyed.

I was filled by that encounter, but I still went to bed that night longing for more. The speaker at the next morning's session was my apostle, Ché Ahn, who pastors HRock Church in Pasadena. I'm sure his message was great, but I don't remember any of it. All I remember is Pastor Ché's reading of the passage in which Jesus asked Mary and Martha, "Did I not say that if you would only believe, you would see my glory?" (See John 11:40.) When I heard that verse, I started to weep uncontrollably because I realized the thing I had been praying for was coming in that moment, simply because I believed. I had read John 11:40 many times before, but, in that moment, God's wind blew on His Word in a fresh way.

Shortly after he read that passage, Pastor Ché concluded his message and released an apostolic blessing over the whole congregation. I was seated in the back of the 400-seat auditorium, since I had arrived late to the session, but when Pastor Ché raised his hands and released the blessing, according to my associate pastor, I was thrown out of my seat against the back wall. I lay there convulsing for an hour after the service ended, as if someone were aiming a Taser at me. I remember lying on the floor, thinking it was over, when I heard someone out in the hallway pray aloud, "Give him more, Lord!" When those words hit my ears, the convulsions became even stronger, and I was knocked to the ground again. I never did find out who shouted in the hallway, and I have often wondered if it might have been an angel.

I was finally able to pull myself together enough to meet Pastor Ché for lunch in the speakers' area. While we were eating, a man named John Arnott joined us. John and his wife, Carol, were then the senior pastors of Toronto Airport Christian Fellowship in Toronto, Canada; today, they head Catch The Fire. It was at their church in 1994 that the Holy Spirit came with such power that a long-lasting revival was launched. Hundreds of thousands of people have traveled to Toronto to be touched by God, and the influence of the Toronto Revival is still being felt throughout the world. The Arnotts are generals in the army of the Lord, and it was our honor just to be able to meet Pastor Arnott, much less talk with him about what God was doing in our church and city.

As we stood up from the lunch table, I sheepishly asked Pastor Arnott if he would mind praying for my associate and me. He lovingly obliged. Just as he started to pray, Roland Baker came into the lunchroom. Roland and his wife, Heidi, oversee Iris Ministries, based in Mozambique. This couple had become burned out in ministry and had been getting ready to call it quits when they journeyed to Canada during the Toronto Revival's outbreak and were miraculously touched by God. They received energy, renewed vision, and fresh revelation. Since then, Iris Ministries has seen over eighty-one people raised from the dead, hundreds of deaf ears opened, and thousands of churches planted in the region. On a number of occasions, while feeding the poor, the Bakers' ministry has come close to running out of food, only to see the rations miraculously multiplied. When Roland and Heidi are doing ministry in a remote village, they routinely first ask for all of the deaf people of the village to gather. Once the deaf people have had their hearing restored, the Bakers preach the gospel. How's that for an introduction? Iris Ministries is a graphic picture of the culture of heaven.

More recently, Roland had been so sick that many were convinced he was about to die. His doctors actually summoned his family to come and say their last good-byes to him. But they just believed God through it all, and God miraculously raised him from his deathbed about a month prior to the Voice of Apostles Conference!

While we were finishing our lunch, Roland walked through the door, full of fire from being healed by God, just as John Arnott was about to pray for us. John introduced us quickly, then asked Roland to join in. As soon as these two men laid their hands on us, the power of God surged through me again, only this time, I saw what seemed to be flames of fire shoot from my feet. Not only did I see them in a vision, but it actually felt as if my feet were on fire.

I lost all decorum as I jumped up and down because I had a "holy hot foot" happening to me.

All that afternoon, I was barely able to function. Later, at the evening session, Winnie Banov, who carries an anointing to bring joy into the darkest of places, laid hands on several of us in the middle of worship time. I found myself laughing uncontrollably. When I finally got back to my hotel room that night and lay down, I noticed I was still convulsing under the power of God.

Ephesians 3:20 teaches us that God goes beyond our wildest imaginations when He provides for us. This was my reality on that day. God had answered a year-old prayer by coming on me with power and joy. He also made it so that modern heroes of the faith would be the ones activating and imparting this unforgettable experience with God in my life. I rarely think about that day without weeping because of the Father's goodness to me. Yet my greatest joy was still awaiting me back home.

CARRIERS OF THE ANOINTING

When the Lord touches a person with a dramatic act of anointing, He causes that person to become a carrier of that anointing. It's as if the person has become infected with a holy "virus" that spreads where the atmosphere is conducive.

I returned home from the conference in Baltimore on Saturday, October 31. Some friends of mine were hosting a harvest party at their home for the children of our church as an alternative celebration to Halloween. I attended the party, and as it concluded, I was asked to pray for all the kids. What an amazing experience. As I prayed for them, one by one, God beautifully touched them, causing them to fall down under His power. Then the parents started asking for prayer, and they started manifesting God's power as well. The living room was full of people laughing with Holy-Spirit joy, the kitchen was full of kids under His power, and the dining room was littered with parents overwhelmed by God.

At our church's Sunday Celebration service the following day, I prayed an impartation prayer, and again the Holy Spirit showed up with extraordinary power. God touched every person who had come to receive prayer.

Not only had God touched me, but I had become a carrier of the Holy Spirit's power.

Let me share a story that truly exemplifies the level of power we experienced that day. One young man in our congregation named Greg, an architect, loved me, and was deeply committed to the ministry I was leading, yet he also considered himself very conservative when it came to matters of faith. He told me later that he came to the front to receive prayer, all the while saying to himself, *I don't want all the "falling down" stuff.*

I like to advise people that whenever they are having someone pray for them, it's best to position themselves to receive, and not to fight any urges to fall, shake, weep...whatever. God's power may manifest in any number of ways, and the one thing people shouldn't do is assume a stance of resistance. Certainly, God can override our objections, but that usually happens when He deems it necessary to get the attention of someone who is not seeking Him. Greg was so adamant about not falling down that he actually put his hands in his pockets to ensure he wouldn't collapse. I have to admit, even my own faith was suspect: As I went to lay hands on him, I said to myself, *There is no way Greg is going down.* I quickly prayed for him before moving on. Having prayed for the next two people, I turned around and saw Greg lying flat on his back, shaking and quivering under the power of God, with his hands still in his pockets.

The "more" I had been searching for had come upon my life, and I have never been the same since. I wonder if I would still be searching and waiting now, had I not been willing to leave my own familiar setting and go get a fresh drink from the Holy Spirit.

NO LIMITS!

Tunnel vision is the main culprit keeping us from accessing other "springs" in the kingdom of God. Unfortunately, many local churches tend toward self-absorption, which locks them into a pattern of thinking that is actually anti-kingdom. When this happens, believers may begin to lose sight of the value of being involved in anything that isn't related to their own "stream," their own tribe, their own church.

Professor Bruce Cook teaches that there are three rungs on the Christian ladder. The first rung is the step where we are concerned exclusively about ourselves. We fixate on what God can do for us. The second rung is church allegiance. People who are intensely loyal to their own church populate this rung. It is good to commit to one's local church; in fact, the church is God's vehicle for bringing individuals to maturity in Christ. But it still isn't the highest level. The third and highest level is commitment to the kingdom of heaven. This was the level that Jesus occupied and from which He taught. He came preaching, "Repent! For the kingdom of God is at hand." (See, for example, Matthew 3:2; 4:17.) Kingdom-level thinking takes us outside the self-centered concerns that so easily consume many believers. It gives us a perspective that encompasses so much more.

The apostle Paul was able to write to the church in Philippi about "thankfulness" and "joy" even while in the pit of prison because he knew that something greater than his own situation was unfolding.

> **GOD IS SO MUCH BIGGER THAN WHAT GOES ON IN OUR OWN CHURCHES AND LIVES. OFTEN, WHEN GOD GRANTS US THE REFRESHMENT WE'VE BEEN ASKING HIM FOR, HE REQUIRES THAT WE GO OUTSIDE THE CAMP.**

God is so much bigger than what goes on in our own churches and lives. Often, when God grants us the refreshment we've been asking Him for, He requires that we go outside the camp. The ten lepers in Luke 17 encountered Jesus outside the city gates. They were deemed unclean by the law and had to live outside the city limits, but it was there that revival and healing broke out. I often wonder if there was anyone in that city who heard that Jesus was doing something great and got hungry enough to run to where He was instead of waiting for Jesus to come to his or her comfort zone.

Sometimes, revival is under way, but it is outside our doors. Accessing it requires stepping outside our normal environment so we can step into what God is doing.

The fact of the matter is that God chooses to manifest His power in different places. Recently, we've seen massive renewals and revival in Brownsville, Toronto, Pasadena, Kansas City, and Redding. These are places where God is moving differently. Some may think, *If God is going to do a thing, then He'll come to where I am if He wants to.* This is not always the case. Oftentimes, He wants us to chase after Him.

The psalmist wrote, *"As the deer pants for the water brooks, so my soul pants for You, O God"* (Psalm 42:1). I can identify with that hunger. I've traveled far and wide to get in on an available anointing that is being released in a distant region because I live with a conviction that nothing else matters but God. God, by Himself, is the greatest reward. I love His benefits—the things He does for me—but, at the end of the day, the things He does for us pale in comparison to who He is, all by Himself. Why He chooses to show up where He does is a question we love to debate, but the fact is, no one can know for sure. Our real concern should be finding where He is and going after what He is giving out, wherever that may be.

When revival broke out in Kansas City, we sent several of the kids from our children's ministry there because we want our children to become God chasers, too.

It is our firm conviction that we should chase after God wherever He can be found, and that there should be no limits on our pursuit of Him.

HAPPY DRUNKS

I have never met a person filled with the Holy Spirit that the world did not consider eccentric.
—*Charles Finney*

The apostle Paul instructed believers not to get drunk on wine, which leads to debauchery, but rather to be filled with the Holy Spirit. (See Ephesians 5:18–20.) In the original Greek, the verb *"filled"* in Ephesians 5:18 is in the present continuous tense. So, Paul was actually instructing us to drink, and to keep on drinking, of the Holy Spirit. Happily, I've discovered this dimension of drinking continually from the wells of revival. I'm happy because it keeps me fresh and also demonstrates my thirst for more of God. I've also discovered it rids me of guilt and shame and keeps me full of joy.

I am an international apostle, but I'm also a local pastor caring for the needs of the congregation I serve. That dual role means I spend a lot of time immersed in the sufferings of people in my home region. Therefore, the call to be continuously filled with the Spirit is vital for me; it is an effective antidote to negativity.

Some church bodies seem to embrace a somber and even mournful disposition as a means of drawing closer to the Father. In their mind, being somber is somehow equated to piety. Pastors and leaders may sense a call from God for the church to go deeper into His presence, but instead of scheduling a series of joyous worship experiences or nights of celebration, they plan solemn assemblies full of gut-wrenching repentance and sorrowful tears. These types of events can actually work against the goal of getting closer to the Father. Sometimes, a heightened awareness of one's failures makes us feel even more distant from God than we already felt.

Don't misunderstand me; there are certainly moments when it is appropriate to be somber and serious. I simply believe that believers practice false humility far too often by adopting solemn dispositions in an effort to get closer to God.

Paul intentionally likened people who become intoxicated due to alcohol (whose drunkenness leads to foolish behavior) to people who get filled up with the Holy Spirit. In effect, Paul was saying, "If you're going to be drunk on something, be drunk on the Holy Spirit, which will lead you to sing songs of Him and His goodness."

People who are drunk on alcohol tend to act without any inhibitions. They often become chatty and flirtatious, trying to hug everyone; they may dance around. Paul was saying that believers should be doing those things, too, except that the fuel for our joyous behavior should not be alcohol but the Holy Spirit.

When we come upon a well of revival, it isn't the time to be mournful or solemn; it's a time to rejoice, a time to dance and make merry in our hearts, because the Holy Spirit who has filled us is the source of true joy and encouragement. So, we get to be happy, holy "drunks" who are full of the Holy Spirit.

WHEN WE COME UPON A WELL OF REVIVAL, IT ISN'T THE TIME TO BE MOURNFUL OR SOLEMN; IT'S A TIME TO REJOICE, A TIME TO DANCE AND MAKE MERRY IN OUR HEARTS, BECAUSE THE HOLY SPIRIT WHO HAS FILLED US IS THE SOURCE OF TRUE JOY AND ENCOURAGEMENT.

On the first day of Pentecost, the religious people thought that the upper-room community was drunk because of the ecstatic euphoria they were displaying. (See Acts 2:5–13.) The apostle Peter had to explain that they were not drunk but full of the Holy Spirit, just as Joel had prophesied. (See Joel 2:28–32.) My contention is that we still need to live with that kind of euphoria, and we can't afford to allow the religious people of our day to reason us out of our joy.

THE JOY OF THE LORD, OUR STRENGTH

When we enter an atmosphere that is charged with the tangible presence of the Lord, the act of drinking in that presence reminds us of how much God loves us. The sense of His presence actually sets up a blockade against the guilt and shame that the enemy wants us to harbor in our hearts, so that we can truly say that the joy of the Lord is our strength. (See Nehemiah 8:10.)

We see in the book of Nehemiah one of the most noteworthy biblical examples of what I'm talking about. Nehemiah was busily heading up the rebuilding of the walls of Jerusalem when the people recovered a copy of the Word of God. The text was brought to Ezra, who began to read aloud to the people. Some had never heard such words, and the anointing on the Scripture was so powerful that they began to weep, because they were overwhelmed with the guilt of knowing they had not been living according to God's Word. However, Ezra and Nehemiah forbade them from mourning because they knew it was not a time for weeping but rather rejoicing. (See Nehemiah 8.)

Can you imagine the scene? Ezra is reading, and the anointing is so heavy that people start to cry because they've never felt or heard anything like it before. Suddenly, their leaders tell them to stop weeping and start rejoicing, for *"the joy of the Lord is your strength"* (Nehemiah 8:10). These leaders were training the people to respond appropriately to the presence of God, and it's a lesson we are still learning today.

In Revelation 12:10, the enemy is called *"the accuser of our brethren."* Satan loves to accuse Christians. The enemy works in the realm of introducing guilt and shame, but the presence of Jesus wars against that, and looks to initiate a celebration of His goodness.

The point is that we're wired to go from glory to glory. (See 2 Corinthians 3:18.) Nowhere in Scripture does the Father condone the idea of His people resigning as they get older. There's an unspoken lie that says the older we get and the longer we've been serving God, the less of an impact we should be making. Retirement may be a legitimate goal when it comes to our vocations, but it should not be so for our spiritual lives. Our hearts must remain alive to God by our drinking continually from the life-giving spring of the Holy Spirit. It is therefore crucial for all believers, young and old alike, to maintain a mind-set of advancement.

When Jesus encountered the woman at the well (see John 4:1–42), that woman was, on the surface, completely disqualified to do anything for God. Because of her gender, she was deemed worse than a second-class citizen. She was also a Samaritan, and Jews traditionally viewed Samaritans as being dirty from the cradle. It's possible this woman had been leading an immoral lifestyle. Yet the Lord invited her to take a drink from Him, with the promise that she would never thirst again. As a result of her encounter with Jesus, not only was this woman freed from her guilt and shame, but her entire city came to know Christ because of her testimony. (See John 4:39.)

Great power gets released in our lives when we decide to stay "well-watered" by the Holy Spirit. There is much we've been given to do, and none of it can be accomplished without the presence and power of the Holy Spirit saturating every cell of our beings. Taking continual drinks from His spring keeps us in a season of perpetual refreshment. And, as we learn from the prophet Isaiah, the act of eating and drinking of God actually brings abundance and satisfaction to our souls:

> *Every one who thirsts, come to the waters; and you who have no money come, buy and eat. Come, buy wine and milk without money and without cost. Why do you spend money for what is not bread, and your wages for what does not satisfy? Listen carefully to Me, and eat what is good, and delight yourself in abundance.* (Isaiah 55:1–2)

8

POWER GIVING

Salvation may be free to us, but seeing the kingdom of God will cost us, at every level—not just financially. In the kingdom of God, finances present a touchy subject, even though money is a subject to which Jesus devoted the majority of His earthly teachings. What I've discovered is that healthy money management is a key not only to seeing heaven invade a situation but also to sustain revival.

Many believers bristle at the mention of money because—let's face it—the media has made such a public spectacle of Christian organizations and leaders that haven't managed money well. In essence, our modern media has seen to it that the few have ruined it for the many. If we're really honest, there have also been many pastors and leaders who have taught on money with a self-serving agenda.

I decided long ago to trust the Lord with our finances, both personal and church related. That decision has given me such freedom and revelation on this all-important topic. We must extend grace to leaders in this area, because in the same way that many people struggle to trust God that they will be able to pay their electric bills, some pastors periodically struggle with trusting God that the payroll of their church will be met. Unlike us, God isn't up and down about the subject of finances, so we should always look to Him for our standard in money management.

Right now, some of you may be asking yourselves, *What does money have to do with the culture of heaven, or keeping the presence of God?* I am what some would call an "external processor," which means I like to think out loud and process thoughts in my head by talking through them. It's the way I'm wired, and maybe you are, too. The opposite would be an internal processor—one of those people who like to mull over things on their own, form a conclusion, and then take action. Regardless of how we identify ourselves, when it comes to the topic of money, we need to settle this issue if we want to experience sustained revival and reformation!

I may have been externally processing in the past, and it may sound as if I'm still doing so in the present, but I'm not. I have come to a conclusion, and that conclusion is this: Stewarding our financial resources wisely and generously is a key to seeing the culture of heaven here on the earth. Or, to use the phrase the Lord gave me, "power giving" is a key to seeing and sustaining authentic revival.

THE PORTAL OF GENEROSITY

> Too often we assume that God has increased our income to increase our standard of living, when his stated purpose is to increase our standard of giving.[21]
>
> —*Randy Alcorn*

One major revelation I have received regarding money and the culture of heaven is that to trigger a move of God, we have to put our money where our mouth is. It's the principle of putting feet to our faith.

---

21. Randy Alcorn, *Money, Possessions, and Eternity* (Carol Stream, IL: Tyndale House Publishers Inc., 1989), 301.

In the Old Testament, the fire of God always fell on the altars that had been built for sacrifice. We may not build altars or burn animal sacrifices anymore, but fire still falls on our sacrifices. More often than not, the sacrifices we New Testament Christians are called to make are financial ones.

In the fall of 2011, the church I was a part of launched a campaign of radical generosity. We determined, as a congregation, to commit random acts of kindness, often by paying to purchase items to cover the needs of others. At restaurants, grocery stores, and gas stations, we looked for opportunities to be radically generous. To our amazement, in the process of our doing this, we noticed God starting to open up the miraculous. Our generosity became a doorway to supernatural encounters.

One evening, my son and I were out grocery shopping and felt led of God to pay for the groceries of the woman in front of us in line. When I asked her if she would allow me to swipe my debit card to pay for her purchases, she looked as if she thought she were being filmed for *Candid Camera*. I explained that I just wanted to show her God's love in a tangible way, and she began to cry.

I instructed my son to help her carry her groceries to her car. By the time we had crossed the parking lot, God had given me some very specific prophetic words about her and her family. I asked if I could pray for her, and in my prayer, I shared those words from God. The woman began to weep once more, and she asked me how it was that I knew about those things. I told her that God simply loved her and had chosen to use me to display His love and affection for her that day. Needless to say, she and her family were at our church the very next Sunday.

HISTORICALLY, WE HAVE LEARNED HOW TO ACCESS THE HEAVENLY REALMS THROUGH PRAYER AND FASTING. I BELIEVE WE HAVE YET TO OPEN UP THE GATEWAY OF GENEROSITY.

What I learned from this encounter is that our generosity can become a portal for God's invasion. Historically, we have learned how to access the heavenly realms through prayer and fasting. I believe we have yet to open up the gateway of generosity, and that, in many cases, heaven doesn't get revealed on earth until we have taken action.

NO RECESSION FOR POWER GIVERS

The apostle James wrote that "*faith without works is useless*" (James 2:20). Power giving is such an effective launchpad into a life of divine encounters. I believe that a generous lifestyle, at the surface level, positions us to partake of the great transfer of wealth that many have prophesied is upon us right now. We're seeing a real economic shift; God is more clearly delineating those who are in Goshen versus those who are in Egypt. (See Exodus 8:22–23.) I am convinced that we're going to start seeing the saved—those who are truly a part of God's kingdom—be spared the effects of recession. We're going to see followers of Jesus come into growth and prosperity, even when times are tough.

The same year that our church began the campaign of radical generosity, a businessman who was participating told me that even though the nation was experiencing a recession, it had been his most successful year after thirteen years in business. How was that possible? It was possible because in the kingdom of God, we live under a different set of rules. The Bible says that God has delivered us, or translated us, out of the kingdom of darkness and into the kingdom of His Son, whom He loves. (See Colossians 1:13.)

When I travel abroad to a nation that is known for instability, one of the first things I like to find out is the location of the U.S. Embassy—not because I'm fearful but because I know global law states that the U.S. Embassy, despite its being geographically located in a foreign nation, is still U.S. soil. My nation's law applies there.

Think about this fact as it relates to the kingdom of God. We live in the world, but we are not of this world. (See John 17:14.) Paul's statement in Colossians 1:13 means that God has translated us out of one culture into another. In the nation of darkness, we are subject to sickness, disease, and financial ruin. However, we are not citizens of that earthly kingdom; we are citizens of another culture, God's kingdom. Thus, even during times of recession, widespread layoffs, or severe budget cuts, we should not allow ourselves to be filled with worry. As people of God, we get to remain in a state of peace because the rules of this fallen world don't apply to us. Believers should therefore never become nervous when discussing money; on the contrary, they should be excited because they think like royalty, and they know that their generosity will return to them tenfold.

We have to mature to the place where we realize we can't have one foot in one kingdom and the other foot in another. We have to understand economics in light of the kingdom of God. This is an area of potential growth for many churches. When I travel to different churches and teach on healing, signs, and wonders, the atmosphere is almost always electric. How different the climate becomes when the subject turns to finances. Even my messages on confronting personal issues have gone over better than my talks on money.

IT SEEMS PEOPLE ARE MORE COMFORTABLE TALKING ABOUT GENERATIONAL CURSES, SEXUAL SINS, AND DEPRESSION THAN THEY ARE ABOUT THEIR MONEY. THIS JUST SERVES TO SHOW HOW MANY ARE STILL LOCKED IN THE "OLD WINESKINS" THINKING.

Today, it seems people are more comfortable talking about generational curses, sexual sins, and depression than they are about their money. This just serves to show how many are still locked in the "old wineskins" thinking. Many Christians still wrestle with a poverty mentality—the mind-set that says, "It is more pious to be poor than to be rich." At some point, we have to bring our concept of money into alignment with the kingdom of God, which we are called to inhabit even now. Living in the kingdom of God makes the discussion about finances a joyous one.

The early church gives us the template for joyous financial freedom. Consider this passage from the book of Acts:

> *All those who had believed were together and had all things in common; and they began selling their property and possessions and were sharing them with all, as anyone might have need. Day by day continuing with one mind in the temple, and breaking bread from house to house, they were taking their meals together with gladness and sincerity of heart, praising God and having favor with all the people. And the Lord was adding to their number day by day those who were being saved.* (Acts 2:44–47)

This text uses the word *"saved,"* which is translated from the Greek word *sozo*—a verb that refers to the complete salvation of a person: mental, physical, emotional, and spiritual. This passage doesn't mention money management directly, but it does indicate that those who believed were practicing generosity with one another and with others. That sounds like a financial dimension of salvation to me.

Power giving creates such gladness in the heart that it perpetuates even more sincere action born of faith. This is what happened in the early church. One person gave, and that inspired even more giving until no one had lack. Power giving was one of the factors that created and sustained the culture of heaven in the first Christian community on earth.

EXTREME GENEROSITY

One of the reasons I'm so committed to power giving is because I know it works. It was because of this concept that we were able to secure a building where we could host the presence of God.

In our first year as a church plant, we met in a local high school. Because our overhead costs weren't too high, we were able to save $85,000 that year. It was an excellent financial start for a new church plant made up of about 100 people.

We were feeling pretty good about ourselves that Christmas season, which was the end of our fiscal year, when I received a letter in the mail from another church requesting a financial gift to help them close on their new church property. They were in need of $15,000 and were sending letters to multiple congregations in hopes of accumulating the amount they needed. My immediate inclination was to send them $1,000. But God had bigger ideas. I reread the letter, and as I prayed about what our church should give, I felt that God was saying, "Meet their goal. Give it all to them."

In that moment, I remembered this principle: Sometimes, you don't see a breakthrough until you give something that really costs you.

I spoke and prayed with several of the other leaders at our church, and we agreed that God's will was for us to give the full amount to the other church. So, we gave a gift that cost us—a check for $15,000. We sowed that check in November 2009. At the time, we had not even really started looking for a building we could call our own.

Shortly thereafter, I went to visit the new building that this other church had closed on. I felt so happy seeing them in their new home, but they didn't make a big deal out of our gift or my presence there. On my way to tour the new facility, I had envisioned their throwing a party or rolling out the red carpet or having me preach, but I received no special treatment. There was no card, no flowers, nothing. I was almost offended, until I remembered that I was after something that God alone could give, and His gift had nothing to do with man's accolades. That's a high value that we all need to embrace.

One month later, a property manager took me to see a building I had driven past and had inquired about. We toured the building, and I remember thinking to myself, *This place would be wonderful, but it's so big, I know it must be way out of our price range.*

Not only did we end up getting the building under budget, but six months after the deal was settled, the property manager said to me, "Troy, I'd had a number of churches that had come and inquired about this building, but when I shook your hand in January of 2010, something about you was different."

He didn't understand exactly what he had perceived, but I sure knew what he was talking about. It was the anointing he had felt, and the anointing makes all the difference. I believe that anointing came as a response to our generosity the month prior.

One of the best stories I have ever heard on this subject is from Pastor Bill Johnson. In one meeting, he was asked to describe the greatest miracle he'd seen. His church in Redding is known for miracles, signs, and wonders, so his questioner probably expected to hear a dramatic story of physical healing. The congregants at Bill's church regularly see wheelchairs emptied, deaf ears opened, cancer healed—all sorts of wonderful things. Bill's answer to the question surprised us all.

"The best story illustrating revival has not involved physical healing at all. A woman went to Starbucks, and the Spirit of the Lord told her to pay for the next person's coffee. So, she paid it forward, and then that woman got to the counter, was ready to pay, and found out that her coffee had been paid for. So, she decided, 'I will pay for the next person's coffee.' And this went on and on and on." Bill reported that the chain wasn't broken for about two and a half hours; people just kept paying for each other's coffee. An incredible spirit of generosity was released in that moment of time.

This is what I mean by "power giving." Why call it "power giving"? The essence of each of these stories is that the power of God is released when the people of God start giving. Few things attract heaven more than the spontaneous expression and explosion of generosity on earth.

FEW THINGS ATTRACT HEAVEN MORE THAN THE SPONTANEOUS EXPRESSION AND EXPLOSION OF GENEROSITY ON EARTH.

In his second letter to the Corinthian church, the apostle Paul commended them for their giving, and communicated the supernatural nature of generosity.

> *He who sows sparingly will also reap sparingly, and he who sows bountifully will also reap bountifully. Each one must do just as he has purposed in his heart, not grudgingly or under compulsion, for God loves a cheerful giver. And God is able to make all grace abound to you, so that always having all sufficiency in everything, you may have an abundance for every good deed.* (2 Corinthians 9:6–8)

From this passage, we learn three basic realities about giving in the kingdom of God.

1. WE LIVE IN A KINGDOM WITH THE LAW OF REWARDS.

We honor God with our giving, and that's reason enough to give. But we can't escape the fact that giving always has a reward attached to it.

I must admit, when I became a Christian, I tithed because I had been taught to do so as a child, but I gave offerings because

I realized, from the Scriptures, how much of a reward came back to those who were generous in their giving. When I read the verse that said I would receive thirty, sixty, and one hundredfold what I had given (see Mark 4:20), the practical man in me got excited about giving.

We find a biblical example of the legitimacy of material motivation in the person of David. When David went to visit with his brothers on the battlefield of Elah, what he saw was horrifying. The giant Goliath, a Philistine, was cursing the God of Israel and His army. David became so upset that he challenged the uncircumcised Philistine to a fight. (See 1 Samuel 17.)

Prior to issuing his challenge, David would have learned that several rewards were in store for the man who defeated Goliath. The man who killed Goliath was to receive the king's daughter as his wife, and he would also be absolved of ever having to pay taxes. (See 1 Samuel 17:25.) This means that David's motivation was not only spiritual but also material, at least in part. David was tapping into the kingdom of rewards. He operated from an expectation that he would be remunerated for his act of service.

The apostle Paul's exhortation in 2 Corinthians 9 carries this same theme. In essence, Paul was saying, "If you will give generously, then you will reap generously." Here, he was incentivizing believers by appealing to this kingdom principle.

In the church, many people become overly spiritual about money management. Being spiritually minded about our finances is important, but it is equally crucial to reflect on the very practical rewards of giving. In the economy of God's kingdom, there are irrefutable laws that operate much in the same way as natural laws. For example, Sir Isaac Newton discovered the law of gravity: What goes up must come down. Scripture teaches us its own set of laws, and chief among them is the law of sowing and reaping: When you sow, inevitably, you will reap. (See Galatians 6:7.) We live in a kingdom that rewards, without prejudice, obedience to its governing laws. Thus, when we give, we can expect to be rewarded.

2. WE HAVE THE FREEDOM TO DECIDE WHAT WE WILL JOYFULLY GIVE.

Again, Paul wrote, *"Each one must do just as he has purposed in his heart, not grudgingly or under compulsion, for God loves a cheerful giver"* (2 Corinthians 9:7). The second key of kingdom giving has to do with personal freedom. God grants us freedom with our offerings—we may decide when, where, and how much to give. This is why Paul told the church not to give under a sense of compulsion.

One of the things that has bothered me in the church is the manner in which offerings are often collected. A pastor or prophet stands up and makes an appeal to the congregation that is neither encouraging nor life-giving but is blatantly manipulative. I've even seen churches confer "anointing" on people in correlation with the amount they gave in the offering. In some instances, churches set up queues in which the people go forward to receive anointing according to how much they had given. The blessings received were based on the amount given, whether a hundred dollars, fifty, twenty, or ten. There are myriad ways in which pastors make their appeals and end up guilt-tripping people into giving—in other words, forcing them to give grudgingly. The problem with this type of manipulation is that it causes people to miss the chance to give as the Bible instructs: cheerfully, not under compulsion, and not grudgingly.

The irony is that the pastors who make these types of appeals normally challenge people to exercise faith as they sow, never recognizing that it is their own unbelief that's fueling their appeal in the first place. Our heavenly Father, in His sovereignty, chose to make us free moral agents, for His intent was that through our freedom, we would choose to love Him, to live like Him. He desires that we be unregulated in our money management, as well. Freedom in what we do with offerings is an essential element to activating the power of God.

GOD DESIRES THAT WE BE UNREGULATED IN OUR MONEY MANAGEMENT, AS WELL. FREEDOM IN WHAT WE DO WITH OFFERINGS IS AN ESSENTIAL ELEMENT TO ACTIVATING THE POWER OF GOD.

If we do not exercise freedom in deciding what to do with our money, then our offerings can't be given by faith; and without faith, the power of God is nullified. God wants to bless our offerings; thus, we must be free to decide to trust Him with our money.

While we should have freedom with our offerings, we are under orders when we tithe, giving 10 percent of our earnings back to God and His kingdom. God calls the tithe holy (see Leviticus 27:30), which means that He has set aside that portion of our money for Himself. The tithe is designated for the storehouse. (See Malachi 3:10.) It is to be brought into our spiritual "storehouse," or the local church or ministry where we receive regular spiritual care. Any amount that we give over and above the tithe is considered an offering. How much of an offering we give, and where, is up to us. Wherever and whatever we give, we must be sure to give cheerfully.

There is a sobering lesson in the Bible about giving honestly and cheerfully, and it's found in the fifth chapter of Acts.

> *A man named Ananias, with his wife Sapphira, sold a piece of property, and kept back some of the price for himself, with his wife's full knowledge, and bringing a portion of it, he laid it at the apostles' feet. But Peter said, "Ananias, why has Satan filled your heart to lie to the Holy Spirit and to keep back some of the price of the land? While it remained unsold, did it not remain your own? And after it was sold, was it not under your control? Why is it that you have conceived this deed in your heart? You have not lied to men but to God." And as he heard these words, Ananias fell down and breathed*

> *his last; and great fear came over all who heard of it. The young men got up and covered him up, and after carrying him out, they buried him. Now there elapsed an interval of about three hours, and his wife came in, not knowing what had happened. And Peter responded to her, "Tell me whether you sold the land for such and such a price?" And she said, "Yes, that was the price." Then Peter said to her, "Why is it that you have agreed together to put the Spirit of the Lord to the test? Behold, the feet of those who have buried your husband are at the door, and they will carry you out as well." And immediately she fell at his feet and breathed her last, and the young men came in and found her dead, and they carried her out and buried her beside her husband. And great fear came over the whole church, and over all who heard of these things.*
>
> (Acts 5:1–11)

Peter rightly told the couple that the land was theirs to begin with, and they had freedom to do with it what they wanted, but this couple gave in such a way as to appear more generous than they actually were. They also did this in an atmosphere of abundant grace. Somehow, their hearts had become corroded. They wanted to get in on the glory, but they couldn't afford to give, or just didn't want to give, all that they possessed, as the others were doing. Instead of being honest with the Holy Spirit—instead of being honest with themselves and trusting that God would honor their half-gift—they feigned giving a whole gift, and the deception cost them their lives.

Maybe the apostle Paul had this story in mind when he told the church in Corinth, "Don't give grudgingly. Don't give under compulsion."

Ananias and Sapphira manipulated their freedom in giving in order to look more pious than they actually were. This type of deception still goes on today. I often wonder how many hearts are corroded because people have not cheerfully given out of their freedom but rather have given grudgingly or, as in the case of Ananias and Sapphira, out of some ulterior motive. Freedom and joy in giving take the practice to a higher level and open undiscovered realms of power.

3. GOD BACKS UP OUR GIVING WITH SO MUCH MORE THAN WE INVEST.

A few years ago, our church observed a forty-day fast from fear. We told our congregation that we wanted them to take risks of generosity for the next forty days. The testimonies we received afterward were inspiring. People had prayed for strangers at the gas station; miracles had taken place in banks; healings were reported. It was a marvelous adventure that greatly increased the faith of our members.

It was during our "fear fast" that I discovered a fascinating aspect of giving that made 2 Corinthians 9:8 come alive in a new way. To review, that verse says, *"And God is able to make all grace abound to you, so that always having all sufficiency in everything, you may have an abundance for every good deed."* As I detailed earlier in this chapter, on one occasion, the Holy Spirit prompted me to offer to pay for the groceries of the woman just ahead of me in the checkout line. My obedience led to an earth-changing revelation that I shared with this woman, and she and her family began coming to our church. As my son and I were driving home after our initial encounter with this woman, I heard the Lord say to me, "Sometimes, it's not prayer that breaks you into miracles; sometimes, it's generosity that opens the door to the supernatural."

That day, I understood at a higher level what Paul was saying in 2 Corinthians 9:8. The grace that God will cause to abound is not just a financial grace; it may be a healing grace, an encouraging grace, a grace for wisdom.

What is grace? Some people define it with an acronym, "God's riches at Christ's expense," or as unmerited favor. But it's so much more than that. God's grace is the supernatural ability of the

Father that enables us to do things we couldn't possibly do on our own, or to be someone we couldn't possibly be on our own.

When we live as power givers, our Father provides whatever is required for the circumstances we are facing, making sure we are amply supplied to succeed as His agents for change.

GUESS WHO'S WAITING?

The great revivalist Smith Wigglesworth was known to say, "If God's not moving, I will move Him."

All through the church, people say they are waiting for God; yet I believe there are many times when God is simply waiting for us.

I've learned that one of the ways we can shift things in the heavenly realm is by performing radically generous acts for others here on earth.

I encourage you to take this kind of risk—to conquer your fear of sacrifice by leading a generous lifestyle. Don't just give someone money and walk away. Give, and then ask God to give you something for that person that money can't buy. Pay for someone's fill-up at the gas station this week. Buy someone a beverage at Starbucks. Pay for someone as you ask the Holy Spirit, "What do You want to supernaturally say to this person? What do You want to do for him or her?"

God wants us to be power givers—people who give with an expectation of rewards to come, people who give out of a sense of freedom and joy, and people who open up portals to God's supernatural ministry by way of their generosity.

Giving generously and cheerfully stirs up God's power because He's made a promise that He is able to make all grace abound to us, so that we may have abundance for every good deed.

If you and I want to see the culture of heaven here on earth, then power giving must become our way of life.

CONCLUSION

I love reading about the power, productivity, and potential of the early church; however, I wouldn't trade living now for living then, even for all the money in the world. We're living in the greatest time the church has ever seen, and we have an incredible opportunity to see the fulfillment of the prayer that God's will would be done on earth as it is in heaven. (See Matthew 6:10.) That's what this book is all about—appropriating the culture of heaven, that we might experience it here on earth. The prophet Habakkuk was correct in declaring that the knowledge of God's glory would cover the earth like the waters cover the seas. (See Habakkuk 2:14.) He saw, with eyes of faith, what you and I have a chance to see in reality: the culture of heaven on earth.

The world resounds with myriad prophetic voices all crying out with the same message: This is a time for souls to be won and nations to be transformed. We are a part of the company of people who will get to see this come to pass. We get to partner with God in His church's finest hour. What a privilege to be alive!

Certainly, darkness has increased, but that is precisely what makes this period of time so exciting. God has told us that the increase in darkness will set the stage for our lights to shine that much more effectively. *"For behold, darkness will cover the earth and deep darkness the peoples; but the LORD will rise upon you and His glory will appear upon you"* (Isaiah 60:2).

Now is a time when God is dispensing more grace, fulfilling more prophetic promises, and raising up kings from the caves. An army is rising that will ascend every cultural mountain and bring heaven to earth. The stories and principles I've shared in these pages were meant to stimulate your thinking about the possibilities that lie before you. This is your time to break out and achieve breakthrough you never thought possible into new, heavenly realms.

In heaven, the culture is right-side up, and God's Word is the Rosetta Stone that unlocks the mysteries of life there. It's our world, as we've come to know it, that's upside down. In heaven, we give to receive more, we become servants to become leaders, and we stay quiet to demonstrate wisdom. These are some of the cultural norms of heaven. Now, more than ever before, there is an invitation from heaven beckoning us to bring its realities into our world. We are the only legal agents through whom this can happen.

When Jesus resurrected, He declared that all authority had been given to Him, so we—His people—are to go and disciple nations. (See Matthew 28:18–20.) He connected the authority He had received with our mission. In other words, He freely gave us the authority He had earned so we could fully complete our assignment.

This is your moment. Whether you're paying for your anointing, discovering people to follow, or learning to use what you have, know that God is with you. He wants you to experience and live under the same conditions He now enjoys—the culture of heaven.

ABOUT THE AUTHOR

Troy Goode grew up in Anderson, Indiana. He began his pastoral career in 1998 as associate pastor of Jubilee Christian Church in Boston, Massachusetts. Later, he helped plant a church in Providence, Rhode Island, and was part of the leadership team there until he was called to Northern California in 2015, where he now serves as the executive pastor of Destiny Christian Fellowship in Fremont, California. Troy holds a BA degree from Howard University, a Master of Ministry degree from Gordon-Conwell Theological Seminary, and a doctorate in Practical Ministry from Wagner University. He and his wife Angela reside in Oakland, California. Troy is a true follower of Christ with a passion to see souls saved, lives changed, and revival come to the body of Christ, not only in Northern California, but throughout the nation and the world.